Coast Guards and Ocean Politics in the Arctic

Andreas Østhagen

Coast Guards and Ocean Politics in the Arctic

palgrave
macmillan

Andreas Østhagen
Fridtjof Nansen Institute
Lysaker, Norway

ISBN 978-981-15-0753-3 ISBN 978-981-15-0754-0 (eBook)
https://doi.org/10.1007/978-981-15-0754-0

This Palgrave Pivot imprint is published by the registered company Springer Nature Singapore Pte Ltd.
The registered company address is: 152 Beach Road, #21-01/04 Gateway East, Singapore 189721, Singapore

Preface

This book is about coast guard, their role in the Arctic, and in ocean politics and resource management more generally. It is based on my years of writing about coast guards, from multiple projects at various institutions. This work started in 2014 at the Norwegian Institute for Defence Studies in Oslo, funded by the Norwegian Ministry of Defence. It continued at the University of British Columbia in Vancouver from 2015 to 2017, related to my doctoral thesis on maritime boundaries and maritime conflict, although this is only slightly related to that work. Finally, work on coast guards was concluded at the Fridtjof Nansen Institute in Oslo from 2017 to 2019, where various projects funded by the Ministry of Defence as well as the Norwegian Research Council enabled me to expand on the topic of coast guards in the Arctic.

This book is predominantly previously unpublished material, although it is also based on previously published articles and reports, albeit presented in a different way and with a new approach. Parts of *Andreas Østhagen. 2016. 'High North, Low Politics Maritime Cooperation with Russia in the Arctic'. Arctic Review on Law and Politics 7 (1): 83–100* and *Andreas Østhagen. 2018. 'Managing Conflict at Sea: The Case of Norway and Russia in the Svalbard Zone'. Arctic Review on Law and Politics 9: 100–123* are here used in Chapters 3 and 5. Further, *Andreas Østhagen. 2017. 'Arctic Coast Guard Forum: Big tasks, Small solutions'. in*

S. Bruns and A. J. Neumann (eds), Maritime Security Challenges: Focus High North. Papers from the Kiel Conference 2016. Kiel, Institute for Security Policy, Kiel University, 3–8. is also made use of in Chapter 6.

Lysaker, Norway Andreas Østhagen

Acknowledgements

This book and the work that it is based on, is only possible because public officials willingly take their time to meet and discuss the range of topics that this book covers. The different coast guard services, and especially the Norwegian Coast Guard, the Icelandic Coast Guard and the United States Coast Guard, have been very forthcoming with sharing of information and willingness to be interviewed. In addition, various foreign and defence ministries in the Arctic countries have also been ready to discuss these topics at length, for which I am very grateful.

There are also a number of people that deserve my acknowledgement and gratitude, having helped me to complete this book. The foundation for this book came through my position at the Norwegian Institute for Defence Studies in Oslo, starting already in 2014. Colleagues such as Paal Sigurd Hilde, Kristine Offerdal, Robin Allers, Håkon Lunde Saxi, Ingrid Lundestad, Ida Maria Oma, Roald Gjelsten, and Rolf Tamnes provided valuable perspectives and guidance. My supervisor at the University of British Columbia, Michael Byers, has also guided me through the intersection of international relations and international law. Further, my colleagues at the Fridtjof Nansen Institute, and especially Geir Hønneland, Svein Rottem, Arild Moe, Øystein Jensen, and Anne-Kristin Jørgensen, have willingly shared their knowledge and experience helping this book take form.

Finally, I must thank my family and friends for their eagerness and support, every time I launch a new project. Especially my wife, Victoria, must endure longwinded discussions and explanations of recent projects. Without such support this would not be possible, and for that, I am truly grateful.

Contents

About the Author

Andreas Østhagen is a Senior Fellow at the Fridtjof Nansen Institute (FNI) in Oslo, Norway, a world leading research institute concerned with international relations, Arctic affairs, and resource management. His research looks at Arctic geopolitics and ocean governance, hereunder maritime disputes and resource management. Østhagen is also a Senior Fellow at The Arctic Institute and an Advisor at the High North Center for Business and Governance at Nord University. He has previously worked for the Norwegian Institute for Defence Studies and the North Norway EU Office in Brussels. Østhagen holds a Ph.D. from the University of British Columbia, an M.Sc. from the London School of Economics and a B.A. from the Norwegian University of Science and Technology.

List of Tables

CHAPTER 1

Facing Arctic Challenges at Sea

Abstract This introduction makes use of an example—the *Elektron*-case—to outline the growing importance of coast guard affairs in the Arctic and more generally across the oceans. What rights do states have at sea? How did these come about? What is the room for international cooperation between different countries on coast guard tasks? Why do states choose to cooperate at sea in the first place? These are the overarching questions tackled in this book and outlined in the introduction. This coincides with three trends being explored in this chapter and the book at large, namely the changes occurring at sea in the Arctic, the increasing demand for international cooperation in dealing with these changes, and finally changes occurring in ocean politics more generally.

Keywords Coast guards · Arctic · *Elektron*-case · Ocean politics · South China Sea

In 2005, fisheries inspectors from the Norwegian Coast Guard boarded the Russian fishing vessel *Elektron* in Arctic waters east of the Svalbard archipelago. The vessel was one of the many Russian trawlers that venture as far north as is possible without reaching the edge of the Arctic sea ice every year to trawl the abundant Arctic fish stocks. *Elektron* had been under surveillance for some time by Norwegian authorities for illegal discarding of fish in the Norwegian Fishery Protection Zone (FPZ) around Svalbard.

A. Østhagen, *Coast Guards and Ocean Politics in the Arctic*,
https://doi.org/10.1007/978-981-15-0754-0_1

During their inspection the two Coast Guard inspectors went on to uncover severe violations, and the trawler was arrested and escorted by the Coast Guard vessel *KV Tromsø* towards the Norwegian mainland for the police to continue with the prosecution.

The captain of *Elektron*, in agreement with its Russian owners, had other plans. Just before entering the Norwegian Exclusive Economic Zone (EEZ) he decided to flee with the two Norwegian fisheries inspectors onboard (Åtland and Ven Bruusgaard 2009, 339). For three days, four Norwegian Coast Guard vessels, as well as a maritime surveillance aircraft and several helicopters, caught up with *Elektron* and closely tailed the trawler as it headed for Russian waters, where Russian Navy vessels were waiting. The Norwegian Coast Guard considered using military force to halt the vessel by boarding it. In the end, bad weather was blamed for not following through with the boarding (Åtland and Ven Bruusgaard 2009, 341). It is also highly likely that Norwegian authorities were concerned with the escalation effects such actions could have vis-à-vis Russia in the Arctic (Fermann and Inderberg 2015, 389, 395).

The *Elektron*-incident was widely publicised, with coverage on Norwegian national television. This was in part a conscious strategy by the Norway authorities to gain sympathy for its policies and ensure public support (Fermann and Inderberg 2015, 374, 390). A new coalition government had entered office in Norway only a month earlier, with the fresh foreign minister Jonas Gahr Støre wanting to prove himself as a deft diplomat while also upholding Norwegian rights in the area. By all definitions this was a 'crisis' for the new government.[1] The incident was unanticipated, perceived as a great threat to the actors involved, within a limited timeframe, and had the potential to cause serious damage in the relations between Norway and Russia. It is significant that this incident did not only concern fisheries management, it also took part in the larger context of the disputed regime concerning Svalbard's maritime zone and security relations between one NATO-member, Norway, and a Russia under President Vladimir Putin intent on re-establishing its Arctic presence.

On October 20, however, the two fisheries inspectors were released to the Norwegian Coast Guard by the Russian Border Service, which had arrived to escort *Elektron* to Murmansk after 'intense dialogue' between

[1]As defined by Holsti (1995, 328).

the Russian and Norwegian governments (Skram 2017, 168). The incident has subsequently become an example of a small-scale dispute well managed between Norway and Russia. As described by former Norwegian Coast Guard Chief Skram, the fact that Norway was considered a decent neighbour by Russia, in tandem with the recognition that there needs to be a rule-based regime concerning fisheries in the Barents Sea, helped the two countries manage this particular crisis (Skram 2017, 171). At the same time, the incident led to questions being asked about the division between civilian and military tasks in the Norwegian Coast Guard, as well as how best to manage such volatile incidents in the future as Arctic maritime activity is set to increase further (Hemner et al. 2007; Inderberg 2007).

Governing Oceans

The *Elektron*-incident highlights what this book is about. Firstly, the Arctic maritime environment is changing. Arctic coastal states are struggling to cope with these changes and how to best respond with adequate public services ranging from search and rescue and oil spill preparedness, to general maritime domain awareness. In addition, protection of sovereign rights (hereunder fisheries inspections) is increasingly needed in Arctic waters. The main, if not only, service responding to these demands is the coast guard. Yet Arctic coast guard structures vary greatly across the northern region in terms of Arctic capacities, institutional set-ups, and mandate along a civilian-military spectrum.

At times coast guards get caught in larger military and geopolitical schemes where their role as a branch of a country's armed forces is integral, as exemplified in the *Elektron*-case. In other instances, the civilian nature of coast guard tasks and mandates simplify and de-escalate incidents at sea that might otherwise have the potential to spiral out of hand. It is this balancing act—vis-à-vis other countries but also internally within a country—that deems the coast guard a particularly interesting actor to study. Especially in an Arctic maritime domain—or more accurately within the multiple maritime domains in the Arctic—undergoing rapid economic, climatic and (geo)political transformation, the coast guard becomes the ultimate gage of how Arctic countries are responding to and dealing with a multitude of complex challenges in the north.

Secondly, as the *Elektron*-incident showcases, Arctic coastal states are dependent on *cooperation* across their maritime boundaries in order to solve new challenges that are arising in the region. This specific incident took place in the context of a larger dispute over maritime zones in the Arctic, albeit one where Norway and Russia had—and have—temporarily agreed to disagree, and more importantly, found a working relationship. This relationship has been built over decades involving a Joint Fisheries Commission as well as informal and formal cooperation between the two coast guard services, and more generally between the two countries. Thus, it is not sufficient to only explore how Arctic states have organised and are adapting their response to Arctic challenges; we must also understand *why* and *how* the same states engage in cooperation both bilaterally and multilaterally in order to jointly solve challenges. By engaging with these issues, we will subsequently be able to better comprehend how Arctic states manage potential disputes at sea in the north, and how these low-level mechanisms dispel notions of the Arctic as an arena for resource wars and geopolitical conflict.

Third and finally, although focus here is explicitly on the Arctic region, it is worth noting that states across the seven seas are forced to devote attention and resources to ocean management. The cases and findings in this book are thus also relevant to an increasingly important debate on how to best manage and govern our oceans in the twenty-first century.

Whereas humans have always used the oceans as a base for resource extraction, marine resources—especially fisheries—are becoming increasingly relevant in the global context and growing in scale (FAO 2016, 3–5). Linked, there is also a widespread reduction in the total biomass of marine resources (Wood et al. 2008; Pauly and Zeller 2016). Further, most marine living resources are transnational in distribution, forcing states to interact regarding their management, or to pursue delimitation of rights and access (Prescott and Schofield 2004, 216). Disputes between states over marine resources have thus been commonplace throughout history (VanderZwaag 1983). Ongoing changes in the oceans also affect states' access and rights to marine resources which are expected to become increasingly scarce, like fisheries, oil and gas, and minerals (Pauly and Zeller 2016; *Economist* 2017). Related to this, the migratory patterns of some fish stocks are changing because of changes in the geophysical marine environment (Allison et al. 2009; Brander 2010; Spijkers and Boonstra 2017). With water temperature and currents changing, conflicts over who gets to fish what, and where, are likely to increase (Pomeroy et al. 2007; VanderZwaag 2010; Spijkers et al. 2018).

In the South China Sea, for example, maritime disputes involving China, Vietnam, the Philippines, Brunei, Taiwan and Malaysia have escalated in recent years, as power relations and other political dynamics change and as marine resources grow in importance and scarcity (Kaplan 2011; Simon 2012; Emmers 2010; Nasu and Rothwell 2014). Similarly, and in focus here, in the Arctic Ocean, the melting of the sea ice and the heightened attention paid to the region have led to a focus on previously neglected maritime disputes in the North (Rothwell 1996; Borgerson 2009; Hoel 2009; Byers 2013; Østhagen 2018). Some of the political attention being given to these maritime domains is undoubtedly the result of the changes occurring at sea, as described here. The expansion in human utilisation of the oceans due to transportation and resource needs, as well as greater awareness of what is occurring at sea from both an economic and science perspective, have resulted in greater attention and value being given to maritime space.

Coast guards play a central role in managing these described changes and conflict potential that arises, in general and in the Arctic specifically. Moreover, states in the Arctic are attempting to device new mechanisms bilaterally and multilaterally to more efficiently manage these challenges and avoid potential mishaps at sea. As a new cooperative mechanism for Arctic Coast Guards was established in 2015 (the Arctic Coast Guard Forum) and we continue to see increase in maritime activity (shipping, fisheries, oil and gas exploration, local transport, tourism) across all Arctic states, this book is essential to practitioners, scholars and students in need of information and overview that goes beyond limited case-studies in the Arctic.

Coast Guards, International Cooperation and Ocean Governance

Today's heightened focus on maritime issues is prompting a quest for new approaches to solve the old question of 'who owns what' at sea. This calls into question the assumption, prevalent in studies of international relations and conflict, that maritime space is more prone to dispute resolution and less to escalation and militarisation, due to its limited salience and intangible importance.[2] Given the increased focus on ocean governance in the Arctic, as well as in more southern waters ranging from the South China Sea to

[2]As Kaplan argues, '[t]he sea, unlike land, creates clearly defined borders, giving it the potential to reduce conflict' (2011, 79). Note the term 'salience', as commonly used in studies of conflict over inter-state issues to describe how much political attention a specific issue attracts. See for example Hensel et al. (2008), Nemeth et al. (2014), and Eiran (2017).

the Mediterranean, this book will explicitly examine coast guards and their challenges. This is not only of relevance to the Arctic, but it can help shed light on more general coast guard challenges and—interlinked—challenges linked to ocean governance, international politics and cooperation across boundaries.

This book has multiple objectives. First, it will answer simple yet complex questions such as: What rights do states have at sea? How did these come about? What is the room for international cooperation between different countries concerning coast guard tasks? Why do states choose to cooperate at sea in the first place?

Furthermore, we will explore how Arctic states are being challenged as their coastal regions and maritime domains are rapidly changing. What is the role of coast guards in managing a new Arctic maritime environment? Why and how does this role vary across different Arctic countries?

Finally, we must examine both bilateral and international cooperation among Arctic states, as they are responding to these new challenges at sea. What are the rationales for, the effects of, and the challenges to such cooperation? What lessons can we draw for ocean governance more generally, at a time when oceans are increasingly on the political agenda?

Focus here is on the six countries that have direct (Russia, USA, Canada, Denmark (Greenland), Norway) or indirect (Iceland) access to the Arctic Ocean, as displayed in Table 1.1. By examining how the role of coast guards in the Arctic as well as how Arctic states engage in bilateral and international cooperation to solve challenges at sea, we can dive into the complexities of Arctic headlines, while also understanding larger geopolitical and governance issues arising in the north. This is linked to the notion of a 'changing Arctic' and a growing body of literature looking at different policy domains and developments in the north.

A such, this is not a theory-oriented book. It aims to provide new empirical knowledge by utilising facts, case-studies, examples and assembling these in new and comprehensive ways in order for the reader to better grasp the changes occurring in the Arctic and the way coast guards function and manage these changes. This book does nonetheless lean on some analytical frameworks, namely those arising from the field of political science, and more specifically international relations. Theory in IR (and social studies at large) is seen as providing crucial guidance through studies of social phenomena, providing a starting point for enquiry (Wendt 1999, 40). The end-goal is also to say something here about why states

Table 1.1 Arctic coast guards

Country	*Name*	*Organization*
Denmark (Greenland)	Søværnet (Navy) (1. eskadre)	Danish Defence
Norway	Kystvakten (Coast guard)	Royal Norwegian Navy
USA	United States Coast Guard (USCG)	Department of Homeland Security
Iceland	Landhelgisgæsla (Coast guard)	Ministry of Justice
Russia	Coast Guard of the Border Service[a]	Federal Security Service (FSB)
Canada	Canadian Coast Guard (CCG)	Department of Fisheries and Oceans

Organisations with responsibility for coast guard tasks and associated institutional structures (simplified)
[a]In Russian: Береговая охрана ПС ФСБ России

cooperate the way they do, and grapple with a normative question; namely how to avoid disputes at sea erupting into outright conflict.

The structure of the remainder of this book is set up to achieve the following:

- first understanding the role of coast guards in the context of states' relationship with the ocean (sovereign rights), how and why states cooperate at sea,
- then looking at the changing Arctic maritime environment and related tasks for Arctic coastal states, before comparing and contrasting the various coast guard structures in the Arctic and how they are adapting to the changing environment they operate in;
- and finally, examining the various bilateral and multilateral cooperation mechanisms that have expanded or arisen in the last decade as Arctic states lean on international cooperation as one way of solving the problems their coast guards are facing.

References

Allison, Edward H., Allison L. Perry, Marie Caroline Badjeck, W. Neil Adger, Katrina Brown, Declan Conway, Ashley S. Halls, Graham M. Pilling, John D. Reynolds, Neil L. Andrew, and Nicholas K. Dulvy. 2009. 'Vulnerability of National Economies to the Impacts of Climate Change on Fisheries.' *Fish and Fisheries* 10 (2): 173–96.

Åtland, Kristian, and Kristin Ven Bruusgaard. 2009. 'When Security Speech Acts Misfire: Russia and the Elektron Incident.' *Security Dialogue* 40 (3): 333–53.

Borgerson, Scott G. 2009. 'The Great Game Moves North.' *Foreign Affairs*, March 25. https://www.foreignaffairs.com/articles/global-commons/2009-03-25/great-game-moves-north.

Brander, Keith. 2010. 'Impacts of Climate Change on Fisheries.' *Journal of Marine Systems* 79 (3–4): 389–402.

Byers, Michael. 2013. *International Law and the Arctic*. New York, NY: Cambridge University Press.

Economist. 2017. 'Getting Serious About Overfishing.' *Economist*, May 27. http://www.economist.com/news/briefing/21722629-oceans-face-dire-threats-better-regulated-fisheries-would-help-getting-serious-about.

Eiran, Ehud. 2017. 'Between Land and Sea: Spaces and Conflict Intensity.' *Territory, Politics, Governance* 5 (2): 190–206.

Emmers, R. 2010. 'The Changing Power Distribution in the South China Sea: Implications for Conflict Management and Avoidance.' *Political Science* 62 (2): 118–31.

FAO. 2016. *The State of the World Fisheries and Aquaculture: Contributing to Food Security and Nutrition for All*. Rome. http://www.fao.org/3/a-i5555e.pdf.

Fermann, Gunnar, and Tor Håkon Inderberg. 2015. 'Norway and the 2005 Elektron Affair: Conflict of Competencies and Competent Realpolitik.' In *War: An Introduction to Theories and Research on Collective Violence*, edited by Tor Georg Jakobsen, 2nd ed., 373–402. New York, NY: Nova Science.

Hemner, Jarl Eirik, Magnar Aukrust, Johan Kr. Øydegard, Olav Myklebust, Malin Soltvedt Nossum, Ole-David Stenseth, Martin Ramsland, and Mette Birkelund O'Connor. 2007. 'Arbeidsgruppen for utredning av oppgave- og myndighetsfordelingen mellom Kystvakten, Politiet og Påtalemyndigheten [Working Group for the Investigation of Tasks and Governance Between the Coast Guard, the Police and the Prosecutor's Office].' Oslo.

Hensel, Paul R., S. McLaughlin Mitchell, Thomas E. Sowers II, and Clayton L. Thyne. 2008. 'Bones of Contention: Comparing Territorial, Maritime and River Issues.' *Journal of Conflict Resolution* 52 (1): 117–43.

Hoel, Alf Håkon. 2009. 'Do We Need a New Legal Regime for the Arctic Ocean?' *The International Journal of Marine and Coastal Law* 24 (2): 443–56.

Holsti, Kalevi J. 1995. *International Politics: A Framework for Analysis*. Engelwood Cliffs, NJ: Prentice Hall.

Inderberg, Tor Håkon. 2007. 'Norsk Kystvakt – Politi eller Forsvar? [Norwegian Coast Guard—Police or Defence?]' *Nordlys*, February 19. https://www.nordlys.no/kronikk/norsk-kystvakt-politi-eller-forsvar/s/1-79-2594494.

Kaplan, Robert D. 2011. 'The South China Sea Is the Future of Conflict.' *Foreign Policy* 188: 76–85.

Nasu, Hitoshi, and Donald R. Rothwell. 2014. 'Re-evaluating the Role of International Law in Territorial and Maritime Disputes in East Asia.' *Asian Journal of International Law* 4 (1): 55–79.

Nemeth, Stephen C., Sara McLaughlin Mitchell, Elizabeth A. Nyman, and Paul R. Hensel. 2014. 'Ruling the Sea: Managing Maritime Conflicts Through UNCLOS and Exclusive Economic Zones.' *International Interactions* 40 (5): 711–36.

Østhagen, Andreas. 2018. 'Geopolitics and Security in the Arctic.' In *Routledge Handbook of the Polar Regions*, edited by Mark Nuttall, Torben R. Christensen, and Martin Siegert, 348–56. Abingdon, UK: Routledge.

Pauly, Daniel, and Dirk Zeller, eds. 2016. *Global Atlas of Marine Fisheries: A Critical Appraisal of Catches and Ecosystem Impacts*. Washington, DC: Island Press.

Pomeroy, Robert, John Parks, Richard Pollnac, Tammy Campson, Emmanuel Genio, Cliff Marlessy, Elizabeth Holle, Michael Pido, Ayut Nissapa, Somsak Boromthanarat, and Nguyen Thu Hue. 2007. 'Fish Wars: Conflict and Collaboration in Fisheries Management in Southeast Asia.' *Marine Policy* 31 (6): 645–56.

Prescott, Victor, and Clive Schofield. 2004. *Maritime Political Boundaries of the World*. Leiden, NLD: Martinus Nijhoff.

Rothwell, Donald. 1996. *The Polar Regions and the Development of International Law: Cambridge Studies in International and Comparative Law*. New York, NY: Cambridge University Press.

Shambaugh, David. 2002. *Modernizing China's Military: Progress, Problems, and Prospects*. Berkeley, CA: University of California Press.

Simon, Sheldon W. 2012. 'Conflict and Diplomacy in the South China Sea.' *Asian Survey* 52 (6): 995–1018.

Skram, Arild-Inge. 2017. *Alltid til stede: Kystvakten 1997–2017* [Always Present: Coast Guard 1997–2017]. Bergen: Fagbokforlaget.

Spijkers, Jessica, and Wiebren J. Boonstra. 2017. 'Environmental Change and Social Conflict: The Northeast Atlantic Mackerel Dispute.' *Regional Environmental Change* 17 (6): 1835–51.

Spijkers, Jessica, Tiffany H. Morrison, Robert Blasiak, Graeme S. Cumming, Matthew Osborne, James Watson, and Henrik Österblom. 2018. 'Marine Fisheries and Future Ocean Conflict.' *Fish and Fisheries* 19 (5): 798–806.

VanderZwaag, David L. 1983. *The Fish Feud*. Toronto, ON: Lexington Books.

———. 2010. 'The Gulf of Maine Boundary Dispute and Transboundary Management Challenges: Lessons to Be Learned.' *Ocean and Coastal Law Journal* 15 (2): 241–60.

Wendt, Alexander E. 1999. 'Social Theory of International Politics.' *American Political Science Review* 94: 429.

Wood, Louisa J., Lucy Fish, Josh Laughren, and Daniel Pauly. 2008. 'Assessing Progress towards Global Marine Protection Targets: Shortfalls in Information and Action.' *Oryx* 42 (3): 340–51.

CHAPTER 2

Maritime Sovereignty, Rights, and Cooperation

Abstract Maritime issues have been climbing the political agendas since the early 2000s. This chapter explores the foundational background for how and why states acquired rights at sea in the first place, and how this fit with various conceptualisations of the maritime domain. It maps how states' rights at sea came about more generally, and how the ocean differs from land in terms of sovereign rights and legal institutionalisation throughout the twentieth century. Concepts such as ocean governance, territorial waters, the EEZ and the continental shelf, as well as UNCLOS (Law of the Sea), are explained and discussed. Finally, this chapter turns to examine how and why states cooperate at sea, based on theories from the field of international relations.

Keywords Sovereign rights · EEZ · Continental shelf · UNCLOS · Maritime boundaries

Maritime issues have been climbing the political agendas of the Arctic states since the early 2000s. Retreating sea ice, changing distribution of marine natural resources, and demand for the same resources have combined to create a 'perfect storm' for research and policymaking. Technological advances and developments in international law, as well as the effects of climate change, are increasingly linked to the ocean and the Arctic. Marine

A. Østhagen, *Coast Guards and Ocean Politics in the Arctic*,
https://doi.org/10.1007/978-981-15-0754-0_2

resource management is influenced by these broader processes in international politics, given the legal and political governance frameworks in which ocean-based resource extraction takes place. Key to the management of the oceans are coast guards.

This chapter will explore the foundational background for how and why states acquired rights at sea in the first place, and how this fit with various conceptualisations of the maritime domain. This will, in turn, allow us to examine how and why states cooperate at sea, and then role of coast guards in the changing Arctic maritime environment (Chapters 3 and 4).

The Growing Importance of Maritime Space

Oceans have been central in the development of civilisations.[1] It has enabled the rapid movement of peoples, goods and ideas between land, and even continents. Mahan and Beresford argued already in 1894 that:

> Control of the sea, by maritime commerce and naval supremacy, means predominant influence in the world; because, however great the wealth product of the land, nothing facilitates the necessary exchanges as does the sea. (1894, 559)

The British Naval Historian Till describes in his book *Seapower* (2004, 6–19) the ocean has four historic attributes: as a resource for human development; as medium of transportation and exchange between peoples and cultures; as a medium for information and the spread of ideas; and as a medium for domination and intrusion.

The difference between land and sea is clear, and the maritime domain has been kept separate from land in our attempts at understanding political and economic development. At the same time, how states viewed and utilised the oceans—and eventually attempted to control and develop a legal order at sea—varied and changed over the last millennium (Benton 2010, 153–54). Albeit crucial in the development of civilisations and later the trajectories of nation states, the importance of the maritime has fluctuated. With the extreme global economic growth across borders and continents that has taken place since the end of the Cold War—often labelled 'globalisation'—maritime space has been ascending in importance.

[1] See Paine (2013) *The Sea and Civilization: A Maritime History of the World* and Steinberg (1999) *Navigating to multiple horizons: Toward a geography of ocean-space.*

As Steinberg (1999, 366) puts it: 'we are now entering an era when [...] human interactions with ocean-space are ever more intense and complex'.

Pinpointing the growing importance of the maritime domain is thus not an original endeavour.[2] A quick read of ancient literature stretching from Greece to Iceland or China reveals prominence of the oceans over the last three millennia. However, since the turn of the millennium, certain global trends have amplified the role of the oceans in international affairs. Hannigan (2017, 8) argues that: '[i]ncreasingly [...] oceans are assuming a higher profile, emerging both as a new resource frontier, a medium for geopolitical rivalry and conflict, and a unique and threatened ecological hot spot'. Technological development, increased seaborne trade, changing marine resource distributions and growing demand for the same resources, as well as climate change effects on the oceans, are factors leading to a renewed focus on maritime space and states' rights and responsibilities within this domain.

All these trends are leading to a new 'era' for maritime issues and maritime space (Hannigan 2017). Of importance here is the greater attention to 'who owns what' at sea. States have rights and duties regarding maritime space, and, as this space gains attention, the delineation of ownership and rights is rising to the fore of domestic and international politics.

Rights and Boundaries at Sea

As states formed, developed, and expanded, the need to define and uphold boundaries became increasingly relevant (Tilly 1990, 131). In the maritime, as opposed to land, conflict over boundaries and sovereignty has more often than not been resolved peacefully through negotiations and arbitration.[3] A key component of this is the development of an international legal regime for the oceans.

In the fifteenth century, philosophers and lawyers such as Grotius (mare liberum—freedom of the seas) and Selden (mare clausum—closed seas)

[2] Keohane and Nye (2012, 75) performed the same task in *Power and Interdependence* from 1977, highlighting all the various ways society's utilisation of the ocean had changed from the 1940s until the 1970s: 'By 1970, however, technology had increased mankind's ability to exploit the oceans' space and resources, thus raising questions of scarcity and stimulating countries' efforts to widen the area under their jurisdiction in order to exclude other countries from the resources.'

[3] See Baker's (2013) instructive thesis on the norm of territorial integrity in the maritime domain.

grappled with questions of maritime ownership. From the eighteenth century up until the twentieth century, a country's maritime zone (territorial waters) was deemed to be a 'cannon shot' from land. This was developed by the Dutch lawyer van Bynkershoek in the early eighteenth century, and later defined as three nautical miles by Italian lawyer Ferdinand Galiami. The League of Nations convened on the matter to codify international law concerning the oceans in The Hague in 1930, but never managed to reach an agreement (Friedheim 1993; Baker 2013).

In 1945, US President Truman declared—inconsistent with contemporary international law—that the natural resources of the continental shelf were under the exclusive jurisdiction of the coastal state. Key to the success of this declaration was not only the US' position of strength after the second world war, but also how the principle entitled *every* coastal state with similar rights, as well as how these sovereign rights did not depend on occupation (Byers 1999, 91–92).

After the Second World War, most states expanded their territorial seas from 3 to 12 nautical miles, whereas Peru, Chile, and Ecuador made claims out to 200 nautical miles in an effort to reap benefits from an expansion in fisheries. Decades of negotiations followed to develop a coherent international legal framework for the oceans and in 1982, states agreed on a comprehensive legal regime as the third United Nations Convention on the Law of the Sea (UNCLOS) was finalised. This provided the legal rationale for states to expand their maritime zones from 12 nautical miles (territorial sea) to 200 nautical miles (what became termed the Exclusive Economic Zone—EEZ), as well as codifying their rights on the continental shelf. This was largely driven by growing awareness of possible marine natural resource extraction (hydrocarbons, fisheries, minerals) and a desire among the states to secure potential future gains (Brown 1981; Friedheim 1993). As of 2019, 167 states have ratified the Convention.[4]

It is central to understand the difference between land and maritime space. Especially the concept of occupation—essential in establishing title to land territory—does not hold relevance in the maritime. Occupation of the continental shelf itself cannot separately lead to acquisition of the territory, contrary to customary law on sovereignty over land territory (St-Louis 2014, 16). Thus, a marked separation between land and maritime has become enshrined, as rights to the latter derive from the former. This was

[4]See https://www.un.org/depts/los/reference_files/chronological_lists_of_ratifications.htm.

codified in the 1958 Geneva Convention on the Continental Shelf, which preserved the prospect of exclusive coastal state jurisdiction over offshore seabed resources (UN 1958).

Delimitation of territory (and rights) on land also rests on the principle that the territory belongs to *one* state, and the central point is to establish which state has the most valid claim. In the maritime domain, however, we accept that *both* states sometimes have valid legal titles to a given area, in which case it becomes a matter of 'reasonable sacrifice such as would make possible a division of the area of overlap' (Weil 1989, 91–92). We are also discussing two different forms of 'rights' by states: '… in contrast to land boundaries which separate sovereignties in their totality, maritime boundaries (with the exception of those of the territorial sea) separate only sovereign rights with a functional, and hence limited, character' (Weil 1989, 93). This latter point is crucial, as what we are discussing with regards to states and maritime space are *sovereign rights* to resources in the water column and on the seabed, not the exclusive right to the whole maritime 'territory' in question.

However, Weil (1989, 93–94) warns against exaggerating the difference between land and sea. The 'entry of security considerations' into the delineating process, as well as a general trend of 'territorialisation' of the 200-nautical mile zone, speaks to the growing importance of the maritime (in 1989), as well as an increasing ability by states to enforce and uphold their rights within this space. Booth (1985) similarly argues that the maritime plays an important—and understated—role for states' projection of power, security, and sovereignty. Till describes oceans as having growing relevance as a dominion of power through two complementary variances of sovereignty: instrumental and expressive. Maritime sovereignty might be integral to the state's survival (the former), or upholding sovereignty over a maritime domain becomes an expression of 'national pride and effectiveness' (the latter) (Till 2004, 289).

Conceptions of the relationship between states and the maritime domain are thus not static. The maritime domain has thus grown from an area of what Ruggie (1993, 165) calls 'shared spaces', to become increasingly legalised internationally, as well as under the jurisdiction of maritime states. Keohane and Nye (2012 [org. 1977], 138) argue that the role of oceans in international affairs has changed: 'as underlying power resources (naval force) became constrained under conditions of complex interdependence, the procedures of international organization became more important.' Booth (1985) predicted that UNCLOS would 'blur the boundaries between land and ocean, leading nations to feel protective and sensitive about their maritime spaces' (quoted in Baker 2013, 152). The role of oceans in international affairs thus changed with the introduction and adoption of UNCLOS.

What this entails for the maritime domain is a transfer of rights from the international society to the individual states, by processes taking place at the international stage. Hurd (1999, 382) deems this the 'institutionalisation' of the norm of territorial sovereignty, which can here also be applied to the oceans. Not only does the invention of a 200-nautical miles EEZ confer new sovereign rights (like access to marine resources), but it also entails responsibilities (like environmental protection, resource management, and presence) that define states' ability to uphold sovereign rights in the maritime (Baker 2013). It is this growing preoccupation (by states) with maritime space that has brought the topic of maritime disputes, ocean space, and marine resource management to the forefront of international politics. The ocean—as a political space—consequently holds two contradictory attributes. On the one hand, the ocean is clearly separate from land, governed by an international legal framework that has institutionalised the rights of all coastal states. On the other hand, the increasing attention given to maritime resources and maritime power projection is leading to the politicisation of the oceans, and thus political dynamics that sometimes resemble those of traditional territorial conflicts over land.

Conflict Potential at Sea

However, despite the growing institutionalisation of states' rights at sea, oceans still constitute natural barriers for human activity. It is—due to its spatial characteristics—a costly domain to operate in for any state, requiring investments in coast guards and/or navies. A complex yet manageable task at land—domain awareness—can be highly challenging at sea (Bueger 2015; Balci and Pegg 2006).

The types of potential sovereignty disputes we are discussing in the maritime are thus manifold. In turn this relates to the crucial difference between sovereign rights (the EEZ and the continental shelf) and complete sovereignty. What Krasner (1999) has termed 'Westphalian' sovereignty, namely the ability to exclude external actors from a given territory, is relevant in the maritime to the extent this exclusion concerns illegal activity by third parties. But at the same time, the right of innocent passage and use of oceans place restrictions on states' ability to enforce this form of sovereignty. States cannot deny passage through their EEZ at all times, they can only deny actors access to marine resources and apply environmental regulation in their maritime zones (according to UNCLOS). This, in turn, gives the maritime domain—at least the full extent of a states' maritime zones—an elusive character, and highlights how the maritime can hold similar *and* different notions of sovereignty. Safeguarding and upholding sovereign rights within a maritime domain is consequently more complex than similar sovereignty enforcement on land. The combination of a costly and challenging domain for human activity, and limited legal foundation for complete exclusion from a state's maritime domain, entail that maritime space holds dissimilar notions of control and management than territory on land.

A feature of disputes at sea has therefore been the ability of states to contain sea-based conflictual events to that specific domain. Clashes at sea—often between *one* state and fishermen from another state—occur rather frequent, without disputes escalating further (Nyman 2013, 6). In other words, disputes and clashes at sea are easier to limit in terms of their wider ramifications. This relates to the disputes themselves being of temporary nature concerning access to fisheries (Salayo et al. 2006); an issue of a seasonal character that is often possible to resolve between the states in question due to its limited salience, tangible nature, and divisibility (Hensel et al. 2008).

Direct clashes at sea between two states, however, tend to be of a more serious character and occur less frequent when states are not in a state of war. Furthermore, when states do clash at sea in peacetime, the purpose is predominantly to protect sovereign rights or uphold trade routes of national value (Till 2004, 275–79).

At the same time, there is no natural law that keeps sea-based conflicts separate, and small-scale disputes do undoubtedly run the risk of escalating beyond their limited realm (Jensen and Rottem 2010). Conflict dynamics can occur at sea as well. Escalation between states by introducing maritime forces and project power is possible in the maritime domain as well as on land. The question is whether a state perceives it as beneficial to escalate an underlying conflict of interests. Based on purely material interests, the sea—albeit plentiful in resources—cannot often be said to hold the same material value as territory on land.

The question, instead, is what larger strategic value a given dispute holds, and whether or not it is deemed purposeful to escalate to achieve a strategic goal that might stretch beyond the immediate dispute at hand. For example, hostile encounters including the use of force have occurred from time to time between the Russian border guard (coast guard) and Japanese fishermen around the Kuril Islands; between Vietnamese and Philippine fishermen and the Chinese coast guard in the South China Sea; between the Norwegian coast guard and Russian fishermen in the Barents Sea; and between the US coast guard and Russian fishermen in the Bering Sea. All these encounters have taken place in the context of a larger maritime dispute concerning access to fishing zones and/or maritime boundaries, albeit with varying degrees of escalation between the parties. Context, in other words, is everything.

The chance of a limited incident at sea concerning the protection of sovereign rights is consequently relatively high, and occurs frequently, between states that are interacting within the framework of a larger maritime dispute. Today, more than half of all maritime boundaries remain unsettled (Ásgeirsdóttir and Steinwand 2016, 10; Prescott and Schofield 2004, 218), prompting a number of contexts where frequent limited incidents occur at sea between states and foreign fishing vessels. Yet these are—generally—kept from escalating beyond the maritime domain itself. Moreover, states' historically limited ability to exert full control over their extended maritime domains creates a paradox: despite the chance of a dispute occurring at sea being relatively high, the chance that the dispute escalates into a larger international conflict is relatively low.

Within this environment, and the increased focus on maritime space, sovereign rights at sea, and maritime disputes, coast guards have emerged as a central actor. Coast guards are states' foremost tool for protecting sovereign rights and enforcing jurisdiction within its maritime domain. Coast guards vary across the world. Each coast guard set-up and division of labour is often tailored to the national and historic circumstances in which they were developed, while they are also often a result of the size of both the country itself (geographically), its population and economy (Østhagen 2015).

In sum, there are multiple factors at play when we are discussing maritime competences and setting up an institution managing a whole range of tasks at sea. There are also more to coast guards than just their immediate role as upholders of law and order at sea. They are being utilised as platforms to initiate and scale up international cooperation between states. To this we now turn, in order to examine how, exactly, states cooperate at sea.

Conceptualising International Cooperation

International cooperation has been promoted as a measure to deal with the challenges arising in Arctic waters.[5] We return to exactly *how* this would occur, and with what limitations, in Chapters 5 and 6. Here, let us engage with *why* states cooperate in the first place, and whether the maritime domain stands out in this regard.

A question that seems to preoccupy most scholars in international studies is: under what conditions can we expect states to cooperate?[6] Rationalist approaches within international relations place emphasis on the goal-seeking rational behaviour of states, driven and constrained by material factors as well as institutional structures.[7] For some of these scholars, conflict is a natural part of international affairs, where states seek to optimise their outcomes vis-à-vis each other in the international system. Cooperation (between states) is inherently a product of conflicting interests and/or policies, which in turn are brought into alignment. Conflict thus provides the platform for potential cooperation.

States are the relevant actors, as they engage in bargaining and cost-benefit calculations according to fixed preferences in line with the 'logic of consequences' (March and Olsen 1998). Institutions—as tools set-up by states to manage potential disputes—are arguably rational design consequences of states' interests and a result of a bargaining process between the same states (Fearon 1998; Koremenos et al. 2001). Scholars thus argue that if the dispute at hand is of material character, it should be easier to reach pareto-optimal solutions where each party accepts a negotiated outcome.[8]

Realists, as a strand of IR theory, have particularly limited belief in the value of cooperation as states seek (material) power to enhance their security, in a relative structural power-balance. Cooperation becomes a limited means to an end, with a restrained life-span and shallow depth (Mearsheimer 1995).

[5] See for example Neffenger (2014) and Norwegian Government and Norwegian Ministry of Foreign Affairs (2014).

[6] The alternative formulation is 'under what conditions can we expect war'.

[7] See for example Fearon (1995), Keohane (1984), Keohane and Nye (2012), Krasner (1983), Mearsheimer (2001), Moravcsik (1997), and Waltz (1979, 1959).

[8] See for example (Vasquez 1995; Hensel et al. 2008).

Institutionalists,[9] on the other hand, have more faith in states ability to cooperate to achieve goals beyond security, as well as a belief in the effects of international cooperation (and its institutions) themselves (Moravcsik 1997). By distinguishing harmony from cooperation and discord, Keohane (1984, 53–54) argues that: '[c]ooperation takes place only in situations in which actors perceive that their policies are actually or potentially in conflict, not where there is harmony'. Discord thus provides the platform for *potential* cooperation. When states cooperate in the international system, they often end up developing an explicit or implicit *international regime*.[10] Regimes help 'improve the contractual environment and thus stabilize cooperation' (Levy et al. 1995, 288).

Alternatively (or additionally), an ideationalist approach takes into consideration ideational factors in international politics.[11] These include the conceptualisation of identity, the role of historical images, and the mutual constitutive and socialising processes that occur among actors operating on an international issue.[12] Crucial to the effects of cooperation is the concept of socialisation. Johnston (2001, 488) sets out the argument by stating that 'actors who enter into a social interaction rarely emerge the same'. Outcomes are thus not only a result of a bargain or negotiation; they are constructed, constituted by actors' interactions. States' interests are not predetermined and/or based on purely goal-seeking behaviour (Hopf 2002; Wendt 1999).

Particularly relevant here is the notion of 'epistemic communities'. Put forth by Haas (1989), it is the notion that a small issue area of international cooperation will be dominated by technical experts who not only represent their own states, but also start to share common beliefs and approaches to solving the problems at hand. 'Regimes are not simply static summaries of

[9] Or 'liberal institutionalism'. As a strand of IR theorising often lumped in under the umbrella of 'neoliberalism'.

[10] Krasner's characterisation of a regime from 1982 has become the go-to definition of it in studies of international cooperation. He defined a regime as 'a set of implicit or explicit principles, norms, rules, and decision-making procedures around which actor expectations converge in a given area of international relations' (Krasner 1982, 2). Regimes tend to—by most definitions—be more specific than international organisations and their related policy areas. Regimes are thus issue-specific, such as 'clean water', 'indigenous rights' or 'sustainable fisheries.'

[11] As outlined by Checkel (2008, 52–53).

[12] See Adler and Barnett (1998), Campbell (1998), Checkel (2005), Hopf (2002), Johnston (2001), and Wendt (1994, 1999).

rules and norms; they may also serve as important vehicles for international learning that produce convergent state policies' (Haas 1989, 377).

A core concern is how to measure and separate various causal mechanisms, given the elusive character of some of the ideational concepts (Lichbach 2009; Bennett and Checkel 2015). It should also be able to prove *how* actors with realist mind-sets are actually *socialised* to forgo these conceptions, using cooperation as the vehicle or mechanism for this socialisation (Johnston 2001, 508–9). As Kelman (1996, 101) argues: '[t]he hallmark of social interaction is that each participant tries to enter into the other's perspective and take the other's role, thus gaining an understanding of the other's concerns, expectations, and intentions'. Kaye (2007, 5) argues that 'diplomacy is not just about producing negotiated outcomes but also about influencing how others think'. In contrast to rationalist literature, conflict resolution within this approach is less concerned with 'resolution', and more concerned with 'transformation' of the actors involved (Lederach 1995, 11–24).

In turn, what do these various conceptions of state participation in international cooperation hold for Arctic coast guards? The key point is that they outline differing (and competing?) ways of understanding *why* states cooperate on certain issues, as well as *what* effect cooperation might have on the states in return. With these pointers, we can aim to better understand Arctic coast guard cooperation. Let us turn towards developments and challenges in the Arctic (Chapter 3), and how Arctic states are responding (Chapter 4).

References

Adler, Emanuel, and Michael Barnett. 1998. *Security Communities*. Edited by Emanuel Adler and Michael Barnett. Cambridge, UK: Cambridge University Press.

Ásgeirsdóttir, Áslaug, and Martin C. Steinwand. 2016. 'Distributive Outcomes in Contested Maritime Areas.' *Journal of Conflict Resolution* 62 (6): 1284–1313.

Baker, James S. 2013. 'International Order in the Oceans: Territoriality, Security and the Political Construction of Jurisdiction over Resources at Sea.' Thesis: Department of Political Science, University of British Columbia. http://legacy.politics.ubc.ca/11946/.

Balci, Metin, and Russell Pegg. 2006. 'Towards Global Maritime Domain Awareness—"Recent Developments and Challenges".' 2006 9th International Conference on Information Fusion, FUSION.

Bennett, Andrew, and Jeffrey T. Checkel, eds. 2015. *Process Tracing: From Methaphor to Analytical Tool. International Encyclopedia of Political Science.* Cambridge, UK: Cambridge University Press.
Benton, Lauren. 2010. *A Search for Sovereignty: Law and Geography in European Empires, 1400–1900.* New York, NY: Cambridge University Press.
Booth, Ken. 1985. *Law, Force and Diplomacy at Sea*. Abingdon: Routledge.
Brown, E. D. 1981. 'Delimitation of Offshore Areas: Hard Labour and Bitter Fruits at UNCLOS III.' *Marine Policy* 5 (3): 172–84.
Bueger, Christian. 2015. 'What Is Maritime Security?' *Marine Policy* 53: 159–64.
Byers, Michael. 1999. *Custom, Power and the Power of Rules.* Cambridge, UK: Cambridge Univeristy Press.
Campbell, David. 1998. *Writing Security: United States Foreign Policy and the Politics of Identity.* Minneapolis, MN: University of Minnesota Press.
Checkel, Jeffrey T. 2005. 'International Institutions and Socialization in Europe: Introduction and Framework.' *International Organization* 59 (4): 801–26.
———. 2008. 'Constructivism and Foreign Policy.' In *Foreign Policy: Theories, Actors, Cases*, edited by Steve Smith, Amelia Hadfield, and Tim Dunne, 71–80. Oxford, UK: Oxford University Press.
Fearon, James D. 1995. 'Rationalist Explanations for War.' *International Organization* 49 (3): 379–414.
———. 1998. 'Bargaining, Enforcement, and International Cooperation.' *International Organization* 52 (2): 269–305.
Friedheim, Robert L. 1993. *Negotiating the New Ocean Regime.* Columbia, NC: University of South Carolina Press.
Haas, Peter M. 1989. 'Do Regimes Matter? Epistemic Communities and Mediterranean Pollution Control.' *International Organization* 43 (3): 377–403.
Hannigan, John. 2017. 'Toward a Sociology of Oceans.' *Canadian Review of Sociology* 54 (1): 8–27.
Hensel, Paul R., S. McLaughlin Mitchell, Thomas E. Sowers II, and Clayton L. Thyne. 2008. 'Bones of Contention: Comparing Territorial, Maritime and River Issues.' *Journal of Conflict Resolution* 52 (1): 117–43.
Hopf, Ted. 2002. *Social Construction of Foreign Policy: Identities and Foreign Policies, Moscow, 1955 and 1999.* Ithaca, NY: Cornell University Press.
Hurd, Ian. 1999. 'Legitimacy and Authority in International Politics.' *International Organization* 53 (2): 379–408.
Jensen, Øystein, and Svein Vigeland Rottem. 2010. 'The Politics of Security and International Law in Norways Arctic Waters.' *Polar Record.*
Johnston, A. I. 2001. 'Treating, International Institutions as Social Environments.' *International Studies Quarterly* 45 (4): 487–515.
Kaye, Dalia Dassa. 2007. *Track Two Diplomacy in the Middle East and South Asia.* Santa Monica, CA: RAND Corporation. http://www.rand.org/pubs/research_briefs/RB9539.html.

Kelman, Herbert C. 1996. 'Negotiation as Interactive Problem Solving.' *International Negotiation* 1: 99–123.
Keohane, Robert O. 1984. *After Hegemony: Cooperation and Discord in the World Political Economy*. Princeton, NJ: Princeton University Press.
Keohane, Robert O., and Joseph S. Nye. 2012. *Power and Interdependence*. 4th-Kindle ed. Boston, MA: Longman.
Koremenos, Barbara, Charles Lipson, Duncan Snidal, Barbara Koremenos, Charles Lipson, and Duncan Snidal. 2001. 'International Organization Foundation the Rational Design of International Institutions.' *International Organization* 55 (4): 761–99.
Krasner, Stephen D. 1982. 'Structural Causes and Regime Consequences: Regimes as Intervening Variables.' *International Organization* 36 (2): 185–205.
———, ed. 1983. *International Regimes*. Ithaca, NY: Cornell University Press.
———. 1999. *Sovereignty: Organized Hypocrisy*. Princeton, NJ: Princeton University Press.
Lederach, John Paul. 1995. *Preparing for Peace: Conflict Transformation Across Cultures*. Syracuse, NY: Syracuse University Press.
Levy, Marc A., Oran R. Young, and Michael Zürn. 1995. 'The Study of International Regimes.' *European Journal of International Relations* 1 (3): 267–330.
Lichbach, Mark I. 2009. 'Thinking and Working in the Midst of Things: Discovery, Explanation, and Evidence in Comparative Politics.' In *Comparative Politics: Rationality, Culture, and Structure*, edited by Mark I. Lichbach and Alan S. Zuckerman, 18–71. Cambridge, UK: Cambridge University Press.
Mahan, Alfred T., and Charles Beresford. 1894. 'Possibilities of an Anglo-American Reunion.' *The North American Review* 159 (456): 551–73.
March, James G., and Johan P. Olsen. 1998. 'The Institutional Dynamics of International Political Orders.' *International Organization* 52 (4): 943–69.
Mearsheimer, John J. 1995. 'The False Promise of International Institutions.' *International Security* 19 (3): 5–49.
———. 2001. *The Tragedy of Great Power Politics*. New York, NY: W. W. Norton.
Moravcsik, Andrew. 1997. 'Taking Preferences Seriously: A Liberal Theory of International Politics.' *International Organization* 51 (4): 229.
Neffenger, Peter V. 2014. 'Testimony of Vice Admiral Peter V. Neffenger Vice Commandant on Implementing U.S. Policy in the Arctic.' House Coast Guard and Maritime Transportation Subcommittee. U.S. Department of Homeland Security.
Norwegian Government, and Norwegian Ministry of Foreign Affairs. 2014. 'Nordkloden'. Nordområdene Statusrapport 2014, Norwegian Ministry of Foreign Affairs, Oslo.
Nyman, Elizabeth. 2013. 'Oceans of Conflict: Determining Potential Areas of Maritime Disputes.' *SAIS Review of International Affairs* 33 (2): 5–14.

Østhagen, Andreas. 2015. 'Coastguards in Peril: A Study of Arctic Defence Collaboration.' *Defence Studies* 15 (2): 143–60.

Paine, Lincoln. 2013. *The Sea and Civilization: A Maritime History of the World.* New York, NY: Vintage Books.

Prescott, Victor, and Clive Schofield. 2004. *Maritime Political Boundaries of the World.* Leiden, NLD: Martinus Nijhoff.

Ruggie, John Gerard. 1993. 'Territoriality and Beyond: Problematizing Modernity in International Relations.' *International Organization* 47 (1): 139–74.

Salayo, N. D., Ahmed M., L. Garces, and K. Viswanathan. 2006. 'An Overview of Fisheries Conflicts in South and Southeast Asia: Recommendations, Challenges and Directions.' *Naga The WorldFish Center Quarterly* 29 (1 and 2): 11–20. http://www.worldfishcenter.org/resource_centre/overview.pdf.

St-Louis, Carole. 2014. 'The Notion of Equity in the Determiniation of Maritime Boundaries and Its Application to the Canada–United States Boundary in the Beaufort Sea.' Thesis: Faculty of Law, University of Ottawa.

Steinberg, Philip E. 1999. 'Navigating to Multiple Horizons: Toward a Geography of Ocean-Space.' *Professional Geographer* 51 (3): 366–75.

Till, Geoffrey. 2004. *Seapower: A Guide for the Twenty-First Century.* London: Frank Cass.

Tilly, Charles. 1990. *Coercion, Capital and European States: AD 990–1990.* 1st Ed. Cambridge, MA: Basil Blackwell.

UN. 1958. Convention on the Continental Shelf, Geneva April 29, 1958.

Vasquez, John A. 1995. 'Why Do Neighbors Fight? Proximity, Interaction, or Territoriality.' *Journal of Peace Research* 32 (3): 277–93.

Waltz, Kenneth N. 1959. *Man, the State, and War.* New York: Columbia University Press.

———. 1979. *Theory of International Politics.* Boston, MA: McGraw-Hill.

Weil, Prosper. 1989. *The Law of Maritime Delimitation—Reflections.* London: Grotius Publications Limited.

Wendt, Alexander E. 1994. 'Collective Identity Formation and the International State.' *The American Political Science Review* 88 (2): 384–96.

———. 1999. 'Social Theory of International Politics.' *American Political Science Review* 94: 429.

CHAPTER 3

Maritime Tasks and Challenges in the Arctic

Abstract The Arctic is changing. Although maritime conditions vary across this vast region, increased activity from state and non-state actors alike are challenging the littoral northern states. This chapter takes a look at the changes occurring in the Arctic, specifically focusing on the contrasts between the North American and European Arctic regions, using Greenland, Canada and Norway as examples. The overall trend has been that the number of maritime vessels has increased steadily since the 1990s, while vessel activity is becoming more complex, diverse, and spread-out. The end of this chapter turns to the need for coast guard tasks and what these entails.

Keywords Arctic · Arctic maritime activity · Shipping · Fisheries · Coast guard tasks

The Arctic is changing. Although maritime conditions vary across this vast region, increased activity from state and non-state actors alike are challenging the littoral northern states. This chapter will look at the changes occurring in the Arctic, specifically focusing on the contrasts between the North American and European Arctic regions. Within these domains there is a marked increase in maritime activity, and thus an increase in the need for coast guard tasks.

A. Østhagen, *Coast Guards and Ocean Politics in the Arctic*,
https://doi.org/10.1007/978-981-15-0754-0_3

Activity Patterns—A Snapshot

In the Arctic, the overall trend has been that the number of maritime vessels has increased steadily since the 1990s. As with climatic conditions, however, the situation varies. At times, the number of vessels decreases, as the sea-ice does not retract as expected, or commercial ventures are postponed or cancelled altogether. Yet, the trends all confer an increased number of vessels, or vessel activity becoming more complex, diverse and spread-out.

Most of this traffic derives from intra-Arctic shipping and destinational shipping in the Arctic in itself. The trans-Arctic sea routes themselves are less relevant for the traffic numbers, as they have yet to become fully operational (Brigham 2013; Office of the Auditor General of Canada 2014; Humpert 2014; Borch et al. 2016b). This does not necessarily mean that all Arctic states are expecting a further increase of traffic in their maritime waters. With steady growth since the turn of the millennium, numbers seem to have stabilised in waters around Greenland and northern Canada, while they are slightly increasing in Alaska, Russia and North Norway. The Danish Ministry of Defence, for example, highlights that it does not expect any further dramatic increase of maritime traffic up until 2027 (Danish Ministry of Defence 2016, 31–32).

However, a higher number of vessels present in the north during the summer months, *in tandem* with increased complexity of the maritime activities undertaken, have led to a new situation for the various Arctic coastal states. Increase in traffic has the potential to increase the number of incidents that require engagement from public assets, as well as an increase in the risk of a severe emergency. Looking at three specific maritime domains in the Arctic—*Canada*, *Greenland*, and *Norway*—can pinpoint some of the ongoing developments and current trends.

In Canada, an ice-free Northwest Passage in the summer months is creating expectations—though not necessarily immediate results—of increased freight traffic and tourism (Evans 2012). The number of ships in recent years that have made use of the complete route during the summer months have varied at very small numbers. In the Canadian Arctic at large, the Canadian Coast Guard estimates an increase from approximately 100–150 vessels in 1990–2005, to 300–350 vessels in 2010–2014 (Office of the Auditor General of Canada 2014, Chapter 3:3). Albeit small in terms of real value, in relative terms this constitute an increase of 300 and 400% in vessel numbers.

Activity is also spread along a vast maritime domain, where only a limited portion traverses the waters between Greenland and Nunavut (Davis Strait and Baffin Bay). Despite this, the Canadian Coast Guard is challenged, as it only takes one serious cruise ship incident to demand rapid and sufficient emergency response. As the ship *Crystal Serenity* traversed the Canadian Arctic in the summer of 2016, debates in Canada raged whether or not these types of adventure cruises should be allowed at all, given the pressure they put on emergency response systems (Schwartz 2016; Byers 2016; McGrath 2016).

Waters around Greenland have experienced similar levels of increase in maritime activity over the last decade. When seismic activity was conducted in tandem with exploratory petroleum drilling in 2010–2011, vessel numbers increased dramatically (Østhagen 2014a). There has also been a steady increase in the number of cruise ships around the world's largest island (Danish Ministry of Defence 2011). In total, vessel activity is a combination of local transport, fisheries, cargo transport, and cruise-ship tourism.

Around 60–100 cruise ship vessels operate in Greenlandic waters annually. While the number might be far less than fisheries and local transport, cruise ships account for the greatest number of passengers, between 20,000 and 30,000 per year (Ingimundarson et al. 2016). It should also be noted that the traffic numbers vary depending on which part of Greenland is examined. Most activity takes place in the south or southwest, as this is where most Greenlanders reside, and ice conditions are less severe. Activity is far more limited in the waters to the north and northeast.

However, these numbers are small compared to the activity in the European parts of the Arctic. In contrast to Arctic waters in northern Alaska, Canada and around Greenland, the Norwegian, Icelandic, and Northwestern Russian Arctic maritime domains are almost ice-free. Climatic conditions are less harsh than in the North American Arctic, and population density is higher.

For example, along the Norwegian Arctic coast, there is considerable industry-related shipping going to and from industrial hubs in North Norway and Northwest Russia. Some of this activity is directly linked to the petroleum industry, operating in the Barents Sea and stretching northwards in the Norwegian Sea. Many of the vessels also come from, or are going to, Murmansk, which is a hub for much of the regional maritime transport in the Russian Arctic (Norwegian Government 2017).

Maritime traffic patterns in the Barents Sea are, however, divided between vessel activity along the Norwegian and Russian mainland and the traffic surrounding the Svalbard Archipelago and Frans Josef Land further north. Svalbard only has a population of 2600, with around 2100 residing in Longyearbyen. While the amount of local traffic is therefore limited, the number of cruise ships has been increasing slightly and the number of annual cruise ship passengers have almost tripled since 1997 (Vold et al. 2013, 32; Norwegian Ministry of Justice 2016, 90). Svalbard is unique in the Arctic context, as it is the only place large cruise vessels can reach as far as 80 degrees north without ice-classification (Borch et al. 2016a, 63). Fisheries around Svalbard as well as in the Barents Sea more generally have also been increasing and constitute roughly 70% of all traffic (Norwegian Ministry of Justice 2016, 104). The movement of stocks has led to more complex fishing vessel patterns, especially when it comes to fisheries to the north and east of the archipelago.[1]

In sum, maritime activity is increasing in the Arctic. Although the trans-polar sea routes might not be the main drivers of increased Arctic shipping, the general trend across the region is more cruise ship activity, more fisheries, and certain large-scale industrial projects—like Yamal LNG in Russia—that drives considerable activity in the surrounding area. The trends highlighted here in Canada, Greenland, and Norway are also mirrored in northern Alaska and Arctic Russia, especially in the northwest of that country (Borch et al. 2016b; Conley et al. 2017; Gosnell 2018). However, we must also recognise the variation in activity patterns between the different parts of the Arctic, related to industrial activity, population patterns, and climatic conditions (presence of sea ice).

Challenges and Tasks

As the number of ships in Arctic waters increase, there is an increase in the risk of an accident occurring. The factors that contribute to a heightened risk of emergencies in the Arctic can be categorised as (1) geographic factors, (2) the lack of infrastructure, and (3) limited information. Geographic factors include the ice conditions, which are increasingly difficult to predict as the ice thaws and areas previously covered by sea-ice are opening. Related factors include low temperatures and the winter darkness. There is a limited amount of infrastructure in the region, given the few human

[1] This also entails snow crab fisheries, which has been increasing in recent years (Østhagen and Raspotnik 2019). The crabs have been moving westwards into the waters surrounding Svalbard and have started to constitute a considerable resource.

settlements and the distances between them. For example, SAR aircraft can take anywhere from 6 to 10 hours to travel from southern airbases before arriving to drop equipment in the Arctic (Goegebeur 2014). Finally, lack of information relates to the understanding of the area in which you operate. There are issues with the use of satellites, making it difficult to perform missions with the precision needed for SAR. Related to this is the fact that great portions of the underwater Arctic geography have yet to be mapped sufficiently (Cohen 2010).

This new reality in the Arctic has spurred demand for presence and capabilities among the Arctic states, whose prerogative it is to deal with these threats and provide emergency response capacity. When fisheries grow in volume, so does the need for regular fisheries inspections. Similarly, other constabulary tasks under the prerogative of police authorities demand constant presence in the maritime domain. In instances where vessels traverse maritime borders, control of these is required. Such tasks, in addition to military actions, are all part of upholding a country's sovereignty in its own waters. At the same time, public assets are needed to respond to immediate incidents, such as the search and rescue of sailors and passengers, or environmental protection due to a spill from a vessel or a platform. Less immediate, but still in response to specific demands, are tasks related to the assistance of navigation and passage (Østhagen 2015; Østhagen and Gestaldo 2015; Mitchell 2013).

Table 3.1 Maritime tasks in the Arctic

Maritime task	*Type of task*	*Mode of task*
Constabulary tasks (*law enforcement, anti-terrorism*, etc.)	Legal	Constant & Responding
Border controls	Legal	Constant
Fisheries inspection	Legal/Environmental	Constant
Sovereignty protection (*involves constabulary tasks and border control, in addition to military actions*)	Legal/Defence	Constant & Responding
Search and rescue	Safety	Responding
Assisting passage and navigation (*including ice-breaking*)	Safety	Responding
Oil spill preparedness and response	Safety/Environmental	Responding

The different types of maritime tasks/challenges becoming more prevalent in the Arctic areas in question (Østhagen 2014b)

In sum, we see a paradox in the Arctic concerning activity and maritime risk. The Arctic states—including those in focus here—have promoted their own northern regions in search of investments and regional development. But this increase in activity is leading to new challenges, or an increase in the number of incidents to manage, in Arctic waters. The multitude of tasks are roughly outlined in Table 3.1. We now turn to the service responsible for these tasks, namely Arctic coast guards.

References

Borch, Odd Jarl, Natalia Andreassen, and Nataly Marchenko. 2016a. 'The Norwegian Waters and Svalbard Sea Areas and Activity Level Up to 2025.' In *Maritime Activity in the High North—Current and Estimated Level Up to 2025*, vol. 1, 39–73. Bodø: MARPART Projects Reports.

Borch, Odd Jarl, Natalia Andreassen, Nataly Marchenko, Valur Ingimundarson, Halla Gunnarsdóttir, Iurii Iudin, Sergey Petrov, Uffe Jacobsen, and Birita í Dali. 2016b. *Maritime Activity in the High North—Current and Estimated Level Up to 2025*, 1–130. Bodø: MARPART Projects Reports.

Brigham, Lawson W. 2013. 'The Fast-Changing Maritime Arctic.' In *The Fast-Changing Arctic: Rethinking Arctic Security for a Warmer World*, edited by Barry Scott Zellen, 1–17. Calgary, AB: Calgary University Press.

Byers, Michael. 2016. 'Arctic Cruises: Fun for Tourists, Bad for the Environment.' *The Globe and Mail*, April 18. http://www.theglobeandmail.com/opinion/arctic-cruises-great-for-tourists-bad-for-the-environment/article29648307/.

Cohen, Tobi. 2010. 'Canadian Rescue Capacity Questioned in the Wake of Arctic Ship Grounding.' *Canada.Com News*, August 29. http://www.canada.com/technology/Canadian+rescue+capacity+questioned+wake+Arctic+ship+grounding/3457291/story.html.

Conley, Heather A., Matthew Melino, and Andreas Østhagen. 2017. *Maritime Futures: The Arctic and the Bering Strait Region*. Lanham, MD: Rowman & Littlefield.

Danish Ministry of Defence. 2011. 'Rapport Vedrørende Placering Af Værnsfælles Arktisk Kommando [Report Concerning the Location of Arctic Command].' Danish Ministry of Defence, Copenhagen. http://www.fmn.dk/nyheder/Documents/Rapport_vedr_placering_af_Værnsfaelles_Arktisk_Kommando.pdf.

———. 2016. *Forsvarsministeriets Fremtidige Opgaveløsning i Arktis* [Future Missions of the Danish Ministry of Defence in the Arctic]. Copenhagen, Denmark.

Evans, Pete. 2012. 'Arctic Thaw Heats Up Northwest Passage Dreams.' *CBC News: Business*, September 13. http://www.cbc.ca/news/business/arctic-thaw-heats-up-northwest-passage-dreams-1.1230437.

Goegebeur, Brynn. 2014. 'Canadian Arctic Search and Rescue: An Assessment.' November. http://www.ruor.uottawa.ca/handle/10393/31976.

Gosnell, Rachael. 2018. 'The Complexities of Arctic Maritime Traffic.' *The Arctic Institute*, January 30. https://www.thearcticinstitute.org/complexities-arctic-maritime-traffic/.

Humpert, Malte. 2014. *Arctic Shipping: An Analysis of the 2013 Northern Sea Route Season*. October 20. Washington DC: The Arctic Institute. http://www.thearcticinstitute.org/2014/10/NSR-Shipping-Report.html.

Ingimundarson, Valur, Halla Gunnarsdóttir, Uffe Jacobsen, and Birita í Dali. 2016. 'The Icelandic Sea Areas and Activity Level Up to 2025.' In *Maritime Activity in the High North—Current and Estimated Level Up to 2025*, Vol. 1, 74–86. Bodø: MARPART Projects Reports.

McGrath, Matt. 2016. 'UK-Funded Ice Breaker in "Elite" Arctic Tourism Row.' *BBC News*, June 17. http://www.bbc.com/news/science-environment-36541583.

Mitchell, James R. 2013. 'The Canadian Coast Guard in Perspective.' A Paper Prepared for Action Canada, Ottawa. August. http://www.actioncanada.ca/en/wp-content/uploads/2013/08/Canadian-Coast-Guard-In-Perspective_EN.pdf.

Norwegian Government. 2017. *Norway's Arctic Strategy: Between Geopolitics and Social Development*. Oslo. https://www.regjeringen.no/contentassets/fad46f0404e14b2a9b551ca7359c1000/arctic-strategy.pdf.

Norwegian Ministry of Justice. 2016. 'Meld. St. 32 (2015–2016): Svalbard.' Oslo.

Office of the Auditor General of Canada. 2014. ' Marine Navigation in the Canadian Arctic.' Report of the Commissioner of the Environment and Sustainable Development. Chapter 3. Office of the Auditor General of Canada, Ottawa.

Østhagen, Andreas. 2014a. *Coast Guard Collaboration in the Arctic: Canada and Greenland (Denmark)*. Toronto: Walter & Duncan Gordon Foundation. http://gordonfoundation.ca/publication/731.

———. 2014b. 'Nye utfordringer i nord: Kystvakten i nordområdene [New Challenges in the North: The Coast Guard in the High North].' Institutt for forsvarsstudier. http://ifs.forsvaret.no/publikasjoner/ifs_insights/insights_14/Sider/osthagen_kystvakter_ins_2_2014.aspx.

———. 2015. 'Coastguards in Peril: A Study of Arctic Defence Collaboration.' *Defence Studies* 15 (2): 143–60.

Østhagen, Andreas, and Vanessa Gestaldo. 2015. *Coast Guard Co-operation in a Changing Arctic*. Toronto: Munk-Gordon Arctic Security Program. http://gordonfoundation.ca/publication/749.

Østhagen, Andreas, and Andreas Raspotnik. 2019. 'Why Is the European Union Challenging Norway Over Snow Crab? Svalbard, Special Interests, and Arctic Governance.' *Ocean Development & International Law* 50 (2–3): 190–208.

Schwartz, Karen. 2016. 'As Global Warming Thaws Northwest Passage, a Cruise Sees Opportunity.' *New York Times*, July 6. http://www.nytimes.com/2016/07/10/travel/arctic-cruise-northwest-passage-greenpeace.html.

Vold, Johan N., Irene W. Basili, Hanna L. Behrens, Liv A. Hovem, Ole Arve Misund, Arild Moe, Gunnar Sander, Turid B. Stemre, and Kirsten Hammelbo. 2013. 'Økt skipsfart i Polhavet: Muligheter og utfordringer for Norge [Increased Shipping in the Arctic Ocean: Opportunities and Challenges for Norway].' Norwegian Ministry of Foreign Affairs. April. Oslo.

CHAPTER 4

Coast Guards in the Arctic

Abstract Coast guards and navies vary across the countries in question. Each set-up and division of labour is tailored to the national and historic circumstances in which they were developed, while they are also often a result of the size of both the country itself (geographically), its population and economy. This chapter looks at what a coast guard entails, why they came about, and explicitly examines six Arctic coast guards: Denmark (Greenland); Iceland; Norway; Canada; USA; and Russia. Summarising these differing structures, this chapter turns to a brief discussion on the notion of an effective coast guard-model in the Arctic and beyond.

Keywords Coast guards · Civilian-military spectrum · Coast guard structures · Arctic

Coast Guards

Coast guards and navies vary across the countries in question. Each set-up and division of labour is tailored to the national and historic circumstances in which they were developed, while they are also often a result of the size of both the country itself (geographically), its population and economy.

The notion of coast guards arose two centuries ago when trade was expanding between countries with the use of commercial shipping and countries were interested in claiming customs revenue from trade to and

A. Østhagen, *Coast Guards and Ocean Politics in the Arctic*,
https://doi.org/10.1007/978-981-15-0754-0_4

from ports, while also providing some form of protection in their waters. Simply put, coast guards tend to be based on the demand of one or two services: the need to extract revenue from trade/control revenue flow and/or a growing public demand for a lifesaving service at sea. Some coast guards were consequently established already in the eighteenth and nineteenth centuries, especially in those countries with large maritime domains and a dependency on maritime trade.

Perhaps the most widely known coast guard service—the United States Coast Guard (USCG)—is also one of the first of its kind, established with the creation of the United States Revenue Cutter Service in 1790 (Ostrom 2012). The current USCG is a merger between the Revenue Service and the United States Life-Saving Service in 1915. In the United Kingdom, the Preventive Water Guard was established in 1809 for the purpose of controlling access and entry to British waterways. By 1822 it was turned into Her Majesty's Coastguard, which today still exist as a civilian service under the Maritime and Coastguard Agency. These two institutions constitute early examples of the coast guard service.

Several other coast guard institutions—civilian or military in character—were established with the extension of extended maritime zones in the period 1960–1980. As states' rights and responsibilities at sea were tremendously expanded as the Law of the Sea-regime was finalised in 1982, most coastal states suddenly found themselves in a situation that required investments in coast guard structures in order to uphold sovereignty at sea (Nyman 2013). Many countries subsequently transformed existing maritime services or established new institutions in order to be present in, and control, this newly acquired maritime space.

Finally, as awareness of changes occurring at sea due to human activity and the increasing relative importance of marine resources, several states have decided to re-organise coast guard services in order to prioritise near-to-coast maritime governance. In China, for example, typical coast guard tasks were handled by the Chinese People's Armed Police Force (PAP) established in 1949 (Shambaugh 2002). By 2013, the maritime branch of PAP was turned into a separate Coast Guard structure, first under the State Oceanic Administration, and then in 2018 back under the PAP (Parameswaran 2019). Several other countries in Southeast Asia, Africa, and Oceania have recently established new coast guard services to better manage challenges related to resource management and environmental concern (Bateman 2003; Vogel 2009; Bueger 2015).

Regardless of the various origin stories, *most* littoral states have some form of coast guard structure of either military or civilian character. These are not always titled 'coast guard' explicitly, although they perform the same types of tasks ranging from search and rescue (SAR) to fisheries inspections and—in some instances—defence tasks.

Denmark/Greenland

Denmark does not have a specific coast guard entity, as the *Royal Danish Navy* (Søværnet) is responsible for providing the services that would normally fall to a coast guard. In the Danish Defence Agreement for the period 1995–1999 it was decided that the responsibility for maritime environmental monitoring and protection should be transferred from the Ministry of Environment and Energy to the Navy for cost-efficiency purposes (Danish Ministry of Defence 1995). This was further consolidated with the agreement for 2000–2004, which also led to the transfer of ice breaker capacity to the Navy (Danish Ministry of Defence 2000). The Navy is thus used by various agencies to carry out search and rescue, navigation assistance, environmental protection, and fisheries inspections, in addition to sovereignty and maritime surveillance.

Today, the Danish Navy is divided into the First and Second Squadrons. While the Second Squadron is focused on foreign operations, the first squadron has responsibility for internal affairs, which includes the northern Atlantic (Greenland) and the North Sea (Faroe Islands). Responsibility for coast guard tasks therefore falls under the first squadron headquarters in Frederikshavn, as well as the newly established Arctic Command in Nuuk, Greenland (Danish Ministry of Defence 2011). The Arctic Command is responsible for overseeing all maritime activity in the waters around Greenland and the Faroe Islands, so that the Danish Navy and the local authorities are in close coordination in crisis situations in the High North. It was set-up to enhance the presence of the Danish defence on Greenland as the demand for this presence increased with the envisioned Arctic 'boom'.

In Greenland, local public resources are further split between the police and defence forces. The various maritime tasks are divided between the Danish and Greenlandic governments, following increased autonomy (home rule) for Greenland in 2009 (Jacobsen 2015). The Danish military still manages tasks in the maritime region beyond the territorial waters. Through its naval and land-based presence in Greenland, the Danish Defence also assists the civil society whenever needed (Kristensen et al. 2012).

The Danish Defence emphasises how they believe that their solution—tasking the military with the whole range of tasks that other Arctic states often divide among various civilian authorities—is the most efficient in the case of Greenland (Danish Ministry of Defence 2016, 54). The presence of *both* the Navy (which acts as a coast guard) and the Greenlandic Police has the potential to enable a division of labour depending on the type, scale, and location of the emergency incident. Yet, as the Danish Ministry of Defence's analysis of future missions in the Arctic from June 2016 emphasises, a capacity gap in the waters surrounding Greenland remains (Danish Ministry of Defence 2016). Neither the Navy nor the local police have the resources or capacities to sufficiently manage the increasing amount of demands in the north.

Iceland

The *Icelandic Coast Guard* (Landhelgisgæsla) is a semi-military institution belonging to the Ministry of Justice. As Iceland does not have a military of its own, the coast guard is central in the Icelandic defence capacities. Up until 2006, the US military had managed the US Iceland Defence Force, operating out of Keflavik Naval Air Station. This exclusive US Defence Force had been present since 1951, established after a joint NATO decision, and predominantly consisted of air and ground defence units. The Icelandic Government was openly disappointed with the US decision to leave, and there have been signs that a limited US force might return in the future, albeit with a temporary presence (White 2006).

The Icelandic Coast Guard constitutes the core of the national and local capacity when dealing with maritime incidents. With around five hundred personnel and the whole range of emergency responsibilities, it is a one-stop shop for maritime emergency response as well as security issues in waters around Iceland (Icelandic Coast Guard 2016a). Beyond that, however, Iceland does not have a local force operating on behalf of civilian or military authorities dedicated to maritime response.

The core challenge for the Icelandic Coast Guard is a limited budget. When the United States left Keflavik, the helicopter capacity in Iceland was markedly reduced. Not tailored to Icelandic SAR, the American helicopters were still an integral part of capacities present in Iceland. In 2016, around

60% of the Coast Guard's budget is spent on the aviation division, managing its SAR helicopters (Icelandic Coast Guard 2016b). It is thus not necessarily the lack of coast guard vessels that constitute a core concern, but the lack of funding for crews to keep the vessels operational, as a considerable portion is spent on airborne capacities.

The demand for this capacity—particularly on land—has also grown as the number of tourists has dramatically increased in Iceland from 2006. In a country with less than 350,000 inhabitants, numbers of tourists have grown steadily from 565,611 tourists in 2011 to 2,343,774 in 2018.[1] The Coast Guard's single surveillance aircraft could be utilised further to a maximum of 1000 hours annually, but was in 2016 only operating at 300 hours per year due to budget constraints (Icelandic Coast Guard 2016b). After the United States left in 2006, the Danes have increasingly become a partner to help fill a capacity gap, and the Danish Defence has considered utilising the aircraft further for domain awareness operations along the east of Greenland. This would serve both the Icelandic Coast Guard's need for continued usage of the aircraft and the Danish Navy's need for improved surveillance around Greenland (Icelandic Coast Guard 2016b).

Norway

The *Norwegian Coast Guard* (Kystvakten) is part of the Royal Norwegian Navy and thus part of the Norwegian Armed Forces. The Coast Guard was established in 1977 based on the recommendations of the Stoltenberg Commission who in 1974 was given the task of exploring possible approaches to exercising national sovereignty in Norwegian waters. The driver for the establishment of the Coast Guard was increasing petroleum and fishing activity in the 1960s and 1970s, in conjunction with the expansion of the 200-mile economic zone at sea in 1976 (Knudsen 2008; Terjesen et al. 2010).

The Norwegian Coast Guard's main task is to enforce Norwegian sovereignty. In addition, the spectrum of tasks covers all the traditional Coast Guard tasks from fisheries inspections to environmental protection and search and rescue, as the Coast Guard is frequently used by other Norwegian public authorities responsible for these areas (Coastal Administration, Customs, JRCC) (Norwegian Ministry of Defence 1997). The

[1] See the Icelandic Tourist Board: https://www.ferdamalastofa.is/en/recearch-and-statistics/numbers-of-foreign-visitors.

Coast Guard has limited police authority, defined in the Coast Guard Act of 1997, and may thus report and investigate offences related to fisheries (Norwegian Ministry of Defence 1997).

These tasks and the law separate the Coast Guard from the regular Navy, as the two institutions perform a different set of tasks. While *Kysteskadren* is located at Haakonsvern in Bergen, the Coast Guard's headquarters (SKYS) is at Sortland, North Norway. The Navy has limited presence in Norway's Arctic waters, beyond annual trips north with a frigate and relevant military exercises that take place in northern waters. The Coast Guard, however, is continuously present in the north, performing a whole range of tasks while also ensuring military presence in northern waters.

Finally, it should be mentioned that the Norwegian Archipelago of Svalbard is a somewhat particular case. Norway was granted sovereignty over the Svalbard archipelago with the Svalbard Treaty, signed in 1920 in Paris, which came into effect in 1925. The Treaty gives all nationals of the signatories the right to live and work on the islands, while it places some limitations on Norway's ability to tax and use Svalbard for military purposes. The latter restriction complicates the use of military equipment, although not when the military is performing civilian tasks. The Norwegian Coast Guard, as well as Navy vessels from time to time, make use of Longyearbyen for bunkering (Norwegian Ministry of Justice 2009, 22–23). The Coast Guard itself constitutes the core public resource in maritime emergency incidents, as it aims to be continuously present in waters around Svalbard. During the summer months, the number of coast guard vessels around Svalbard ranges between two and five, whereas this is slightly reduced in winter months.

Canada

The *Canadian Coast Guard* (CCG) is a special agency under the Department of Fisheries and Oceans (DFO). Civilian coast guards often fall under the department of justice (or equivalent) and therefore have legal authority, yet this is not the case in Canada. The CCG is a civilian agency without military capabilities and constabulary tasks such as law enforcement and border control are not mandated to the Canadian Coast Guard, unless it teams up the federal police. The same goes for monitoring illegal fishing and management of marine resources, mandated to Fisheries Officers from the Department of Fisheries and Oceans, which sometimes make use of Coast Guard vessels in their work. Consequently, the structure of the CCG is a limited agency model, mandated to perform only parts of national Canadian maritime tasks that include search and rescue and environmental response.

The Canadian Arctic falls under the responsibility of the CCG's Central and Arctic region, which covers the provinces of Ontario and Quebec, in addition to Nunavut and the Arctic coastline of Yukon and NWT. Search and rescue operations in the Eastern Arctic are the responsibility of the Joint Rescue Coordination Centre (JRCC) in Trenton, Ontario, with the exception of the Southern portion of Baffin Island (JRCC Halifax).

In Canada, the sheer size of the coastal area and lack of physical presence throughout the northern territories make operating in the Arctic a major challenge (Office of the Auditor General of Canada 2014, 3–6). As a remedy, the Canadian Coast Guard (CCG) establishes forward operating bases between May and November when the ice thaws and traffic increases (Varga 2013). The Canadian Coast Guard has in particular been challenged by ageing equipment and reduced ice-breaking capacity—crucial in a Canadian Arctic context due to the presence of sea ice (Francis 2013). Investments have been made to provide the Royal Canadian Navy with Arctic patrol ships and the CCG with a new icebreaker, in order to handle the demands for presence in the Arctic (Byers 2012; Berthiaume 2013; Østhagen 2014, 13; 2015).

United States

The *United States Coast Guard* (USCG) is a separate branch of the US Armed Forces, organised under the Department of Homeland Security in peacetime and can be transferred to the Department of the Navy by the President or the US Congress during times of war. Constituting one out of seven uniformed services in the United States, the USCG is the only branch of the armed forces that has a law enforcement mandate. The tasks of the USCG ranges from environmental proception and search and rescue, to maritime security and defence tasks when needed.

Like the Norwegian Coast Guard, the USCG is charged with enforcing various maritime laws and regulations through a civilian mandate, while also being part of a military structure. In contrast to the Norwegian Coast Guard, the USCG is an expansive government institution on its own, with more than 40,000 workers on active duty and more than 200 vessels (US Coast Guard 2014; Ostrom 2012). This is naturally not only linked to the

Arctic, but to the lengthy US coastline and the various maritime zones in the Atlantic and Pacific Oceans.

The Arctic holds a relatively small place in the USCG daily workings. It is the USCG's 17th district—headquartered in Juneau, Alaska—that is tasked with all of Alaska's maritime domain, including the northern parts stretching from the Bering Sea/Strait into the Chukchi Sea and the Beaufort Sea. There have been concerns in the United States that the USCG has been underfunded and in need of more Arctic-specific investments, such as icebreakers (Conley et al. 2017). The recommended solution by the USCG is found in greater investments in capabilities such as new Polar Security Cutters and a greater focus on enhancing maritime domain awareness (Østhagen 2019).

The USCG—like any branch of government—has its own policy interests vis-à-vis the Arctic. What is unique in the US context is that the Coast Guard clearly articulates these in a public Strategy document. No other Arctic coast guard service—from the Russian FSB to the Norwegian Kystvakten or the Canadian Coast Guard—has produced a similar document or has used such a strong independent voice for promoting its own concerns in the Arctic. This speaks not only to the uniqueness of the US system where the various government institutions enjoy considerable independence: it also speaks to the position and stature of the USCG as the primary branch of the US government that engages with Arctic issues on a daily basis (Østhagen 2019).

Russia

The *Russian Coast Guard* (Береговая охрана Пограничной службы ФСБ России) belongs to the Russian Border Guard Service, which is under the Federal Security Service. During the USSR it was the maritime unit of the KGB Border Troops. Established in its present form in 2007, the Russian Coast Guard is an armed service, although not organised under the Russian Armed Forces, with a mandate to enforce law and use force when needed (Åtland and Ven Bruusgaard 2009; Åtland 2015). The reorganisation in 2007 with the establishment of an independent coast guard service can be seen as a Russian desire to professionalise and de-militarise Russian coastal jurisdiction across vast maritime domains (Åtland 2015, 12). In addition to enforcing law at sea, the Russian Coast Guard's tasks include environmental protection, search and rescue, and fisheries inspections, along the lines of the other multi-purpose coast guards examined here.

The Russian Coast Guard is further organised according to 36 regional border directorates covering the longest national land border in the world, where almost half have a maritime domain or maritime zones connected.[2] As with the USCG, the Russian Coast Guard holds a large number of vessels (estimates vary from 200 to 500 vessels[3]), although many of these are remnants from Soviet times and the capacities and standardisation varies.

Russia holds approximately half of all national maritime space in the Arctic under its jurisdiction, stretching from the Norwegian border and maritime boundary in the Barents Sea to the Bering Strait/Bering Sea in the Far East region. The Russian Coast Guard has—alongside the Northern Fleet and various Arctic military units—been part of a Russian re-invigoration in the north aimed at restoring Arctic capacities to resemble those of the Soviet era, while also tackling new challenges arising from increased traffic along the Northern Sea Route and further ice-melting in the north (Konyshev and Sergunin 2014; Hønneland 2016). The Coast Guard has consequently become a core element in Russia's new strategic and economic focus on the Arctic, through investments in new vessels tailored made for Arctic operations and coast guard tasks such as fisheries inspections and search and rescue, alongside establishment of new FSB/Coast Guard bases in Murmansk and Arkhangelsk (Sergunin and Konyshev 2014; Staalesen 2019).

The various structures are summarised in Table 4.1. The mandates and structures of coast guards vary as the respective maritime areas in each country differ, and dissimilar operational conditions require coast guard specifications to meet national needs. As Norwegian waters are generally ice free, the Norwegian Coast Guard for example does not provide ice-breaking services, although it acquired its first modern vessel with advanced ice-breaking capacity in 2001 (*KV Svalbard*). Where Norway has no heavy icebreaker capacity due to limited maritime activity in the ice-covered waters north of Svalbard, Russia, and Canada has plenty, albeit with ageing fleets. In the United States debates are ongoing on how to best increase its icebreaking capacities in tandem with greater demand for

[2]See http://ps.fsb.ru/regions.htm for a map of Russian border directorates.

[3]See Åtland (2015, 15).

Table 4.1 Coast guards services in the Arctic

Country	*Name*	*Organisation*	*Civilian/Military*
Denmark (Greenland)	Søværnet (Navy) (1. eskadre)	Danish Defence	Military
Iceland	Landhelgisgæsla (Coast guard)	Ministry of Justice	Semi-military
Norway	Kystvakten (Coast guard)	Royal Norwegian Navy	Military
Canada	Canadian Coast Guard (CCG)	Department of Fisheries and Oceans	Civilian
USA	United States Coast Guard (USCG)	Department of Homeland Security (in peacetime)	Military/semi-military[a]
Russia	Coast Guard of the Border Service[b]	Federal Security Service (FSB)	Semi-military

Organisations with responsibility for coast guard tasks and associated institutional structures (simplified)
[a]The USCG is part of the US Armed Forces. Yet, it is dissimilar from the Navy and the Danish/Norwegian counterparts operating under Navy structures. As such, institutionally it straddles the categories of 'military' and 'semi-military'—a category broad in scope, which entail military attributes/affiliation, yet operating distinct from the military in peacetime
[b]In Russian: Береговая охрана ПС ФСБ России

presence by the USCG in the northern parts of Alaska. Around Greenland the Danish Navy's area of maritime presence decreases during winter, as the ice-breaking capacity is limited and general traffic decreases. Coast guard fleets are consequently tailor-made for national needs, whereas other military forces are—to varying degrees—designed to handle more flexible conditions (Bateman 2003; Vogel 2009).

For instance, constabulary tasks such as law enforcement and border control are not mandated to the Canadian Coast Guard, unless it teams up the federal police in Canada. In Norway, however, the Coast Guard has limited police authority due to a special legal act from 1997—*Kystvaktloven* (Norwegian Ministry of Defence 1997). It can therefore operate on behalf of the full range of appropriate public authorities, like the Coastal Administration or the Customs Services. As the responsibility for coast guard tasks around Greenland falls to the Royal Danish Navy's first squadron, the Navy's responsibilities have come to include search and rescue and environmental protection, in addition to traditional sovereignty enforcement (Table 4.1).

In sum, the six coast guard structures in question are varied, ranging from a civilian to a military model, with various parent-organisations and different operating environments, both in the Arctic and more generally. The most effective way to organise Arctic coast guard tasks is not given, and in some countries there have at times been strong voices questioning their chosen model. In Canada there have been debates on whether the Coast Guard or the Royal Navy should be prioritised for Arctic operations, while some have argued for making the CCG a branch of the Navy (Francis 2013; Byers 2012). In Denmark, the growing awareness of the importance of the Arctic, and more specifically the prospects of oil and gas production in Greenlandic waters, have led to arguments for a new civilian structure tasked with maritime environmental protection (Holm 2012a). In a reversal from the debate occurring in Canada, there have been arguments from Danish politicians for separating the coast guard's tasks from the Navy (Holm 2012b). In Norway the structure and mandate of the Coast Guard has often been highlighted as a cost-efficient and credible solution to the tasks at hand (Knudsen 2008; Terjesen et al. 2010, 455–89). Yet, there have been voices arguing for a civilian coast guard to handle the new challenges in the north and to specialise in the type of tasks that are growing in demand, like oil spill preparedness and search and rescue (Henriksen 2007).

Consequently, there are almost as many coast guard models as there are coast guards, each specified to national demands and the larger institutional set-up in which they adhere. Despite all these domestic debates, coast guard structures seem unlikely to change in the near future and will remain relatively dissimilar. The question is what effect these structures have on their respective countries' ability to handle new challenges in the Arctic, and what they entail for further cooperation across (maritime) boundaries in the north, topics to which we now turn.

References

Åtland, Kristian. 2015. 'Den Russiske Kystvakten Mot 2020—Organisering, Kapasiteter Og Operativ Virksomhet.' *FFI-Rapport*. Kjeller: Norwegian Defence Establishment (FFI).

Åtland, Kristian, and Kristin Ven Bruusgaard. 2009. 'When Security Speech Acts Misfire: Russia and the Elektron Incident.' *Security Dialogue* 40 (3): 333–53.

Bateman, Sam. 2003. 'Coast Guards: New Forces for Regional Order and Security.' In *Analysis from the East-West Center*. January. Honolulu: East-West Center.

Berthiaume, Lee. 2013. 'Coast Guard's New Icebreaker to Cost Twice as Much as Originally Estimated.' *Canada.Com*. http://o.canada.com/news/coast-guards-new-icebreaker-to-cost-twice-as-much-as-originally-estimated.

Bueger, Christian. 2015. 'From Dusk to Dawn? Maritime Domain Awareness in Southeast Asia.' *Contemporary Southeast Asia: A Journal of International & Strategic Affairs* 37 (2): 157–82.

Byers, Michael. 2012. 'You Can't Replace Real Icebreakers.' *The Globe and Mail*, March 27. http://www.theglobeandmail.com/globe-debate/you-cant-replace-real-icebreakers/article534351/.

Conley, Heather A., Matthew Melino, and Andreas Østhagen. 2017. *Maritime Futures: The Arctic and the Bering Strait Region*. Lanham, MD: Rowman & Littlefield.

Danish Ministry of Defence. 1995. *Aftale Om Forsvarets Ordning 1995–1999* [Agreement on the Defence 1995–1999]. Copenhagen: Danish Ministry of Defence.

———. 2000. *Forsvarsforlig 2000–2004* [Agreement on Defence 2000–2004]. Copenhagen: Danish Ministry of Defence. http://www.fmn.dk/videnom/Pages/Tidligereforsvarsforlig.aspx.

———. 2011. *Rapport Vedrørende Placering Af Værnsfælles Arktisk Kommando* [Report Concerning the Location of Arctic Command]. Copenhagen: Danish Ministry of Defence. http://www.fmn.dk/nyheder/Documents/Rapport_vedr_placering_af_Værnsfaelles_Arktisk_Kommando.pdf.

———. 2016. *Forsvarsministeriets Fremtidige Opgaveløsning i Arktis* [Future Missions of the Danish Ministry of Defence in the Arctic]. Copenhagen: Danish Ministry of Defence.

Francis, Diane. 2013. 'Canada's Navy: Deep-Sixed Over the Decades.' *Huffington Post Canada*. http://www.huffingtonpost.ca/diane-francis/canada-navy_b_3641651.html?utm_hp_ref=tw.

Henriksen, Torstein. 2007. 'Militær eller sivil Kystvakt?' *Nordlys*, October 29. http://www.nordlys.no/debatt/ytring/article3087873.ece.

Holm, Erik. 2012a. 'Eksperter og fagfolk vil samle maritime opgaver i en kystvagt [Experts and Practitioners Want to Gather Maritime Tasks in One Coast Guard].' *Ingeniøren*. http://ing.dk/artikel/eksperter-og-fagfolk-vil-samle-maritime-opgaver-i-en-kystvagt-134968.

———. 2012b. 'Regeringspartier positive over for Dansk Kystvagt [Government Parties Positive to Danish Coast Guard].' *Ingeniøren*. http://ing.dk/artikel/regeringspartier-positive-over-dansk-kystvagt-135103.

Hønneland, Geir. 2016. *Russia and the Arctic: Environment, Identity and Foreign Policy*. London: I.B. Tauris.

Icelandic Coast Guard. 2016a. 'Icelandic Coast Guard—Always Prepared.' About Us. http://www.lhg.is/english/icg/about-us/.

———. 2016b. 'Icelandic SAR and the Coast Guard.' Reykjavik: Interview by Andreas Østhagen.

Jacobsen, Marc. 2015. 'The Power and Paradoxes of Collective Identity Narration: Greenland's Way to a More Autonomous Foreign Policy (2009–2014).' *Arctic Yearbook.* https://arcticyearbook.com/arctic-yearbook/2015/2015-scholarly-papers/127-the-power-of-collective-identity-narration-greenland-s-way-to-a-more-autonomous-foreign-policy.

Knudsen, Willy. 2008. 'Fra fiskerioppsyn til Kystvakt - en studie av en beslutningsprosess [From Fisheries Inspections to Coast Guard: A Study of a Decision-Making Process].' *Det Samfunnsvitenskapelige Fakultet.* Tromsø: University of Tromsø.

Konyshev, Valery, and Alexander Sergunin. 2014. 'Is Russia a Revisionist Military Power in the Arctic?' *Defense and Security Analysis* 30 (4): 323–35.

Kristensen, Kristian Søby, Rune Hoffmann, and Jacob Petersen. 2012. *Samfundshåndhævelse i Grønland: Forandring, Forsvar Og Frivillighed.* Copenhagen, Denmark: Centre for Military Studies, University of Copenhagen. http://cms.polsci.ku.dk/cms/samfhaand/Samfundsh_ndh_velse_i_Gr_nland.pdf/.

Norwegian Ministry of Defence. 1997. 'Lov Om Kystvakten (Kystvaktloven) [Law Concerning the Coast Guard].' Forsvarsdepartementet. http://lovdata.no/dokument/NL/lov/1997-06-13-42.

Norwegian Ministry of Justice. 2009. 'St. Meld. Nr. 22 (2008–2009): Svalbard.' Oslo.

Nyman, Elizabeth. 2013. 'Oceans of Conflict: Determining Potential Areas of Maritime Disputes.' *SAIS Review of International Affairs* 33 (2): 5–14.

Office of the Auditor General of Canada. 2014. 'Report of the Commissioner of the Environment and Sustainable Development: Marine Navigation in the Canadian Arctic.' Edited by Office of the Auditor General of Canada, Chapter 3. Ottawa: Office of the Auditor General of Canada.

Østhagen, Andreas. 2014. 'Coast Guard Collaboration in the Arctic: Canada and Greenland (Denmark).' Toronto: Walter & Duncan Gordon Foundation. http://gordonfoundation.ca/publication/731.

———. 2015. 'Coastguards in Peril: A Study of Arctic Defence Collaboration.' *Defence Studies* 15 (2): 143–60.

———. 2019. 'What the New US Coast Guard Strategy Tells Us about the Arctic Anno 2019.' *High North News*, April 25. https://www.highnorthnews.com/en/what-new-us-coast-guard-strategy-tells-us-about-arctic-anno-2019.

Ostrom, Thomas P. 2012. *The United States Coast Guard and National Defence: A History from World War I to the Present.* Jefferson, NC: McFarland.

Parameswaran, Prashanth. 2019. 'Managing the Rise of Southeast Asia's Coast Guards.' Washington, DC. https://www.wilsoncenter.org/sites/default/files/2019-02_managing_the_rise_of_southeast_asias_coast_guards.pdf.

Sergunin, Alexander, and Valery Konyshev. 2014. 'Russia in Search of Its Arctic Strategy: Between Hard and Soft Power?' *Polar Journal* 4 (1): 69–87.

Shambaugh, David. 2002. *Modernizing China's Military: Progress, Problems, and Prospects*. Berkeley, CA: University of California Press.

Staalesen, Atle. 2019. 'New FSB Base Opens Way for More Operations in Arctic.' *The Barents Observer*, January 3.

Terjesen, Bjørn, Tom Kristiansen, and Roald Gjelsten. 2010. *Sjøforsvaret i Krig og Fred: Langs Kysten og på havet gjennom 200 år* [The Navy in War and Peace: Along the Coast and at Sea Through 200 Years]. Bergen, Norway: Fagbokforlaget.

US Coast Guard. 2014. *Daily Chronology of Coast Guard History*. Edited by United States Coast Guard. August. Daily Chronology: United States Coast Guard. http://www.uscg.mil/history/Chron/Chronology_Aug.asp.

Varga, Peter. 2013. 'Iqaluit Coast Guard Office Maintains Pan-Arctic Vigil.' *Nunatsiaq Online*. http://www.nunatsiaqonline.ca/stories/article/65674iqaluit_coast_guard_office_maintains_pan-arctic_vigil.

Vogel, Augustus. 2009. 'Navies Versus Coast Guards: Defining the Roles of African Maritime Security Forces.' In *Africa Security Brief*, vol. 2 (December). Washington, DC: Africa Center for Strategic Studies.

White, Josh. 2006. 'U.S. to Remove Military Forces and Aircraft from Iceland Base.' *The Washington Post*, March 17. http://www.washingtonpost.com/wp-dyn/content/article/2006/03/16/AR2006031601846.html.

CHAPTER 5

A Case of Bilateral Cooperation: Norway–Russia

Abstract There are more to coast guards than just their immediate role as upholders of law and order at sea. They are also being utilised as platforms to initiate and scale up international cooperation between states. This chapter explores Arctic cooperation on maritime issues, looking at an example of bilateral coast guard cooperation by examining the most in-depth case to-date, namely between Norway and Russia. Despite being on opposite sides concerning security interest (NATO–Russia), these two neighbours have managed their ongoing disputes through low-level cooperation on coast guard and maritime affairs. This can in turn help us better understand the Arctic governance system in general, as well as why the role of coast guards is on the rise in northern waters.

Keywords Russian Coast Guard · Norwegian Coast Guard · Svalbard · Fisheries · NATO · Bilateral cooperation · Barents Sea

Coast guards in the Arctic are few and far between. Current investment levels and equipment do—at times—not match the proclaimed goals of Arctic policy documents. There has thus developed a so-called capability-expectations gap,[1] which has been duly critiqued in recent years (Brigham

[1] Coined by Christopher Hill (1993) to describe the growing expectations concerning the EU's weight as an international actor, this term holds relevance here in describing the gap

A. Østhagen, *Coast Guards and Ocean Politics in the Arctic*,
https://doi.org/10.1007/978-981-15-0754-0_5

2013; Funston 2014). Yet, there are more to coast guards than just their immediate role as upholders of law and order at sea. They are also being utilised as platforms to initiate and scale up international cooperation between states.

This chapter and the next will explore various low-level Arctic cooperation on maritime issues, looking at examples of bilateral coast guard cooperation by examining the most in-depth case to-date namely between Norway and Russia, before—in the next chapter—exploring the trend of multilateral cooperation between all Arctic states. This can in turn help us better understand the Arctic governance system in general, as well as why the role of coast guards is on the rise in northern waters.

Norway and Russia in the Barents Sea

The Barents Sea is located north of the Norwegian and Russian mainland, just off the Arctic Ocean itself. The maritime area covers approximately 1.4 million square kilometres (540,000 square miles). Its boundaries are set by the Svalbard archipelago (Norway) to the west, Franz Josef Land (Russia) to the north, Novaya Zemlya (Russia) to the east, and the European continent (mainland Norway and Russia) to the south. The Sea is named after the Dutch explorer Willem Barentsz, who ventured northwards in search of a sea route to Asia via the northern hemisphere in the late sixteenth century.

In the post-World War II period, Norway and Russia have been on opposing sides with regards to security and military alliances. Norway has hinged its security on membership in NATO and its bilateral relationship with the United States, with Russia perceived as the primary security challenge (Tamnes 1997; Neumann et al. 2008). For Russia, albeit important given the NATO–Russia relationship, Norway constitutes just one out of several neighbours where security issues might arise (Holtsmark 2015). The Barents Sea has been central in the relationship between these two countries. It is a maritime domain integral to the security of both states, as well as to regional economic development in North Norway and Northwest Russia respectively.

between the expectations of booming Arctic maritime activity and the inability of coast guards to manage potential incidents at sea.

When Norway and Russia established their 200 nautical mile exclusive economic zones (EEZs), in 1976 and 1977 respectively, a dispute concerning the maritime boundary between the two countries in the Barents Sea arose. The size of the disputed area was approximately 175,000 square kilometres. An agreement concerning the disputed area, the 'Grey Zone Agreement', was signed in 1978 and was renewed annually up until 2010. The agreement recognised the countries' rights to fisheries in the area, without tackling the legal dispute itself. In 2010—after 33 years of negotiations—Norway and Russia agreed on a joint maritime border more or less dividing the disputed area in half (Henriksen and Ulfstein 2010, 1–2).

The waters around the Svalbard archipelago is a somewhat different story. Norway was granted sovereignty over the archipelago with the Svalbard Treaty, signed in 1920 in Paris, which came into effect in 1925. The Treaty gives nationals from the signatory countries the right to live and work on the islands, while it places some limitations on Norway's ability to tax and use Svalbard for military purposes (Svalbard Treaty 1920). The latter restriction complicates the use of military equipment, yet not when the military is performing civilian tasks. The Norwegian Coast Guard makes use of Longyearbyen for bunkering and other civilian purposes. Similarly, although the Norwegian Government has restricted the use of Longyearbyen airport to civilian aviation only, military aircraft can use it when performing civilian tasks such as search and rescue and oil spill response (Norwegian Ministry of Justice 2009, 22–23).

After establishing its EEZ in the Barents Sea in 1976, Norway decided to establish a Fisheries Protection Zone (FPZ) around the Svalbard Archipelago in 1977. Norway argues that the 200-mile maritime zone around Svalbard is subject to Norwegian sovereign rights (Jensen 2014, 102). Other countries, however, claim that the principles of the Svalbard Treaty should apply to the 200-mile zone, even though only territorial waters were explicitly stated when the Treaty was formalised in 1920. This reading of the Treaty would require that Norway under articles 2 and 3 cannot discriminate between Norwegian nationals and nationals of the other signatories when it comes to economic activity in the maritime zone. A third approach is to claim that neither the Treaty nor Norwegian rights apply to the zone, in turn deeming the zone around the archipelago international waters (Pedersen and Henriksen 2009).

To avoid an outright challenge to the Norwegian claim, and to protect and manage what is the central nursery area for the Northeast Arctic cod stock, the Norwegian government established the FPZ in 1977 (Jensen

2014, 103). So far the other Treaty signatories have accepted this, although Russia and Iceland in particular have been outspokenly critical of what they perceive of as discrimination towards their fishing vessels by the Norwegian Coast Guard (Molenaar 2012; Pedersen 2009, 2017; Hammerstrøm 2015).

In terms of economic activity, the Barents Sea is the breeding and nurturing place for the largest cod stock in the world, the Northeast Arctic cod, which has been one of the main reasons for subsistence along the North Norwegian and Northwest Russian coasts (Hønneland 2013, 21). The Sea is also rich in a number of other marine species that have fostered economic activity, like shrimp, whale, seal, and of late, king and, increasingly, snow crab (Østhagen and Raspotnik 2019).

Establishing Bilateral Maritime Cooperation

In the 1970s, cooperation between Norway and Russia in the Barents Sea developed pragmatically in response to the establishment of the EEZs and the subsequent disputes that arose. An agreement between Norway and the former USSR on fisheries in the Barents Sea was completed in 1975, and the first Joint Fisheries Commission between the two countries convened in 1976. The Commission's role is to ensure sustainable management and exploitation based on scientific advice of the four stocks that are considered common in the Barents Sea, namely Northeast Arctic cod, haddock, capelin, and Greenland halibut (Byers 2013, 40; Hønneland 2013, 24–25). This has become the primary mechanism to solve—or at a minimum manage—disputes concerning fisheries in the Barents Sea.

Since 1979, seismic surveying and exploratory drillings have also taken place in the Barents Sea. On the Norwegian side, Statoil has produced LNG from the Snøhvit gas field since 2006, and ENI started production of oil from the Goliat field in 2016. Offshore activity on the Russian side has been at a lower level, as there are more easily accessible commercial resources to extract onshore/near offshore in the Yamal/Nenets region further east (Claes and Moe 2014, 102–10). As petroleum exploration in the Barents Sea expanded and the Cold War ended, Russia and Norway agreed on an oil spill agreement in 1994, which included developing joint contingency plans and procedures for notification in the event of an oil spill (Stokke 2000). Search and rescue cooperation was initially based on an agreement from 1956, which was renewed in 1988 and 1995 (Eie 2011, 6–7).

Practical cooperation between Norway's and Russia's coast guards started in the early 1990s (Østhagen 2016; Hønneland 2012a). After the Soviet Union collapsed, fishing vessels started overexploiting the Barents cod stock and in 1992 the Joint Fisheries Commission expanded their mandate to include control measures. Routines for sharing information on catches were subsequently established (Hønneland 2013, 38). By 2000, cooperation had further developed and a Memorandum of Understanding outlining a number of cooperative measures was signed between the countries and their coast guards (Norwegian Directorate of Fisheries 2013). An additional—and substantial—part of the coast guard cooperation involves the mutual exchange of fisheries inspectors and operational personnel. Central to this cooperation is that coast guard personnel thus meet with their Russian or Norwegian counterparts to learn procedures, exchange experiences and establish personal relations.

In sum, these various measures of relatively in-depth cooperation have derived from the need to jointly manage fish stocks in the Barents Sea to the benefit of both Norway and Russia. As such, maritime cooperation expanded to deal with a growing number of challenges: initially the increase in unregulated fisheries and subsequently a wide range of tasks relating to search and rescue, oil spill prevention and response, and management of marine resources. The Joint Fisheries Commission in particular is a central tool for managing fisheries between the two countries, often described as the backbone of bilateral cooperation in the Barents Sea (Hønneland 2012b; Stokke 2014; Henriksen and Ulfstein 2010).

With an increase in northern maritime traffic, the coast guards are forced to devote more resources to handling potential challenges. As fisheries grow in volume, so does the demand for fisheries inspections conducted by the coast guards on behalf of their national authorities. As the number of cruise liners increase, so does the need for systems that can handle a potential search and rescue incident. Similarly, in ice-covered parts of the Arctic (in this case in Russia), the demand for aid to navigation—sometimes requiring ice-breaking—has increased (Mitchell 2013; Østhagen 2015). These challenges have prompted a desire to explore mutually beneficial arrangements in the Barents Sea, as elsewhere.

Managing Conflict?

Despite these positive traits in the bilateral cooperation, complete harmony does not prevail between Norway and Russia in the Barents Sea. Albeit well managed, there have been incidents in the Barents Sea that have had the potential to escalate and take on the characteristics of a 'crisis'. Tensions between Norway and Russia have arisen in connection with Norwegian arrests of Russian vessels in the FPZ, and the potential escalation that can occur from a fisheries incident to a state-state incident.

It is customary that Russian fishing vessels inspected by the Norwegian Coast Guard in the FPZ refuse to sign the inspection documents as a gesture to highlight Russia's refusal to recognise Norwegian authority in the Zone—although they allow the Norwegian Coast Guard to perform inspections of the vessels (Kosmo 2010; Jørgensen 2010). The Russian Coast Guard has, on occasion, suggested that Norway and Russia conduct joint fisheries inspections in the FPZ around Svalbard (Ege 2012). Such cooperation would, however, challenge Norwegian sovereignty and authority in the FPZ, and the Norwegian Government has declined all such proposals (Østhagen 2015, 2018).

Up until the turn of the millennium, Norwegian enforcement of fisheries regulation in the FPZ was relatively constrained compared to the Norwegian EEZ (Skram 2017a, 159). In the late 1990s, however, scientists reported that fish stocks were in decline and quotas had to be reduced to achieve sustainable fisheries (Hønneland and Jørgensen 2015, 61; Skram 2017b). Calculations show that in the period 2002–2005 alone, Russian fishing vessels exceeded their quotas in the Barents Sea by around 100,000 tons annually (Skram 2017a, 163).

At the same time, the Norwegian Coast Guard Act (*Kystvaktloven*) was passed in 1997, with an increased focus on competence enabling measures in the Coast Guard (Norwegian Coast Guard Official I 2017; Skram 2017b). From around 2000 onwards, there was a shift in enforcement policy in the FPZ. Increased competence in the Coast Guard in combination with growing concerns over the state of the fish stocks, led to stricter enforcement of the regulatory regime (Hønneland and Jørgensen 2015; Skram 2017b; Norwegian Coast Guard Official II 2017). As has been documented by Østhagen (2018), a number of incidents arose from 2001, some of which led to verbal confrontation between Norway and Russia.

In March 2014, Russia annexed Crimea, and relations between Norway and Russia became strained as Norway followed the EU and the United States sanctioning Russia over its actions in Ukraine. In the Barents Sea, the biannual exercise Northern Eagle between the USA, Norway, and Russia was cancelled in 2014. Similarly, the bilateral military naval exercise Pomor, between Norway and Russia, was also cancelled. This exercise had been reconvened back in 2010, to highlight how the armed forces in Norway and Russia could jointly solve challenges arising in the Arctic (Lysvold 2010).

However, after an initial halt in cooperation, relationships on coast guard affairs quickly resumed normality. In the Barents Sea, the Norwegian authorities placed considerable emphasis on the importance of continuing cooperation and dialogue with Russia, as relations grew tense (Jacobsen 2014). Cooperation on coast guard affairs, border guard services, and emergency response were upheld, while dialogue between the Chief of the Russian Northern Fleet and the Chief of the Norwegian Joint Military Headquarters still continued on a weekly basis (Østhagen 2016). The 'Barents'-exercise, which targets coast guard and rescue tasks specifically, similarly continued to take place.

In terms of consequences for disputes related to Svalbard, it is hard to pinpoint exact effects. As the Norwegian Coast Guard highlights, the larger international dispute has not had any direct effect on Norway–Russia cooperation concerning coast guard affairs in the Barents Sea (Norwegian Coast Guard Official I 2017; Norwegian Coast Guard Official II 2017).

At the same time, there has been an increased amount of attention given to the potential for conflict in the Barents Sea (Østhagen 2016). Both countries deem this to be a region of significance, as highlighted by a report by the Russian Defence Ministry in 2017 listing Svalbard and its maritime zone as potential areas for confrontation between Russia and NATO (*Aftenposten* 2017; Nilsen 2017). Following that report, a controversial Norwegian blog concerned with defence—aldrimer.no—reported that Russia had simulated an invasion of Svalbard during its military exercise *Zapad* in 2017 (Stormark 2017). Albeit not surprising given Russian military strategies in the north (Gade and Hilde 2015), this was refuted by both the Norwegian Minister of Defence and the Head of the Norwegian Military Intelligence Service (Lindi et al. 2017). Whether or not it was accurate, it sparked a brief debate amongst Norwegian politicians and defence analysts and highlights the underlying fear that Svalbard might become an arena for conflict with Russia.

Enabling Successful Bilateral Coast Guard Cooperation?

A more stringent enforcement of regulations in the FPZ was pursued from 1998 onwards, whereas Russia has at times responded to arrests by the

Norwegian Coast Guard with diplomatic protests and a show of military force. In some instances, the arrest of a single trawler has also spilled over into the Joint Fisheries Commission and hampered cooperation. It seems, given the two countries' willingness to use force (or the threat of the use of force), that the conflict at large and the incidents on their own have the potential to escalate from a win-win situation to a situation where one or both parties stand to lose.

Specifically concerning the attempted arrests of *Chernigov* in 2001, *Elektron* in 2005, and *Sapphire II* in 2011, the arrests themselves *and* the larger issue concerning Norwegian rights in the FPZ, escalated to the extent that threats were implicitly stated through military actions, while certain actors were outspokenly critical of the other party. At least, this was the case among Russian fishermen and their related shipowners, as well as amongst former fisheries officials and regional representatives in Murmansk.[2]

At the national level, however, statements from both Norway and Russia have been constrained. Despite Russian complaints against Norwegian actions in the FPZ, these have not escalated beyond rhetoric and statements (Åtland and Ven Bruusgaard 2009). Therefore, although fluctuating as arrests have occurred, the overarching dispute has not escalated too far towards action, making it manageable for both the Russian and the Norwegian governments.

Asking *why* this is the case, however, is a harder nut to crack. If we return to the initial conceptions of why and how states engage in cooperation and resolve conflict, we can identify some key factors underpinning the relatively stable relationship between Norway and Russia concerning the FPZ. First, rationalist ideas of power, coercion, and interests help frame the FPZ in the larger context between these two states and their regional and global positions. Norway's membership in NATO and outspoken policy of ensuring US support in case of sovereignty threats (Expert Commission 2015), come into play. Yet, deterrence does not help explain *how* and *why* Norway and Russia continue to establish new forms of low-level cooperation in the Barents Sea, and how the two countries solve incidents when they do occur. We therefore must move from the systemic level to the immediate issues at hand between the two actors.

According to rationalist logic, cooperation can be the product of discord. In other words, states cooperate when they disagree. The solution

[2] As described by Åtland and Ven Bruusgaard (2009) and Hønneland (2016, 103–26).

might not only be limited to cooperation within the field of disagreement, but recognition that sometimes formalisation and institutions are needed to overcome the 'self-help' tendencies of the international system. Along this line of argumentation, cooperation between Norway and Russia concerning shared fish stocks, oil spill response, search and rescue, and ship traffic management are formalised arrangements set up to manage potential areas of dispute (Hønneland 1999). Similarly, the Barents Sea maritime boundary agreement in 2010 was a result of interests between the two states converging sufficiently (Moe et al. 2011).

In other words, the reason why Norway and Russia manage to keep crises from escalating further, is mutual interest in preserving aspects of their cooperation; cooperation that benefits both parties. This relates to multiple issue areas. Concerning resource management, Russia is assumed to be satisfied with the current quota scheme, in contrast to what might be achieved if an actual debate over the status of the FPZ took place (Hønneland and Jørgensen 2015). Concerning the UNCLOS-regime, both parties benefit from a stable legal regime in the FPZ specifically, but also in the Arctic at large (Moe et al. 2011). And concerning national security, both parties have an interest in low levels of conflict for fear of coercive efforts by other actors within and outside the Barents/Arctic region (Tamnes and Offerdal 2014).

The interests that drive cooperation might, however, be subject to change (over time). We can see changes taking place within all the issue areas addressed: as climate change continues to alter the marine resource base in the Barents Sea; as external actors challenge the validity of the UNCLOS-regime in the Arctic; or as the power relations between various actors fluctuate. The institutions set up to manage cooperation are also challenged and questions of institutional resilience become salient: how will cooperative mechanisms adapt as conditions influencing the premise for cooperation change (Young 2010)?

For example, as Norway and Russia struggled to reach agreement on a reduction of annual quotas for the Barents Sea in the early 2000s, several institutional measures were taken. In 2002, a harvest control rule was introduced in the Joint Fisheries Commission to set quotas according to scientific advice while also limiting fluctuations from year to year. This has been described as the most important change in the work of the Commission, removing a source of friction between the two states (which had spill-over effects into the FPZ) (Hønneland and Jørgensen 2015, 66). Another adaptation (or innovation) was the development of a port state control regime amongst the North East Atlantic coastal states, which improved information concerning quotas and port deliveries, removing accusations of overfishing and unreliable information (Hønneland and Jørgensen 2015, 62). Similarly, the measures taken in 2012 to harmonise rules for inspections of fishing vessels that were taken after the *Sapphire II* incident removed another source of friction in the FPZ (Skram 2017a, 204).

The rationalist approach to dispute management in the international domain provides a functional answer: institutions are set-up for a purpose and will (must) adapt as conditions for their existence alter. The reason *why* Norway and Russia have managed to avoid further escalation of potential crisis in the FPZ—without settling the overarching dispute concerning the status of the maritime zone—is because their interests have—in theory—converged sufficiently within several related domains and issue areas. If interests remain converged, and/or institutions like the Joint Fisheries Commission can enable convergence through negotiations, incidents are unlikely to escalate into actions that can threaten the larger bilateral relationship.

These explanatory approaches do not, however, capture the whole proverbial elephant. As emphasised by officials in the Norwegian Coast Guard (Norwegian Coast Guard Official II 2017; Norwegian Coast Guard Official I 2017), former Coast Guard officers (Skram 2017b; Government Official Norway I 2017), and multiple scholarly works written on the management of shared fish stocks in the Barents Sea (Hønneland and Jørgensen 2015; Hønneland 1999, 2012a), the individual *personal* level constitute a core element of conflict management in the Barents Sea. This concerns ideational factors, meaning the influence and importance of ideas and social interactions, on top of what we can observe through interest alignment and rational bargaining theory (Checkel 2008).

In the Svalbard Zone, some key elements stand out. The importance of dialogue during a crisis is given much of the credit for solving incidents between the Norwegian Coast Guard and Russian fishing vessels. This includes communication between the Coast Guard and Russian trawlers (including the use of Russian interpreters); between the Norwegian Joint Military Headquarters and the Chief of the Russian Northern Fleet at Severomorsk; and between the negotiating groups in the Joint Fisheries Commission (Government Official Norway I 2017; Skram 2017b). Having various means of communicating, and keeping channels open as a crisis is unfolding, constitute central elements in the management of conflict in the FPZ (Norwegian Coast Guard Official I 2017; Norwegian Coast Guard Official II 2017).

This concerns the larger concept of personal relations, as social contact between two or more individuals representing different sides in a dispute. The theory of socialisation emphasises not only the communication component, but also the fact that a *change* occurs between the parties. Norms (expected behaviour) socialise (change) actors according to a logic of appropriateness (Johnston 2001; Checkel 2005). By interacting regularly with the same individuals on the same issues (fisheries, quotas, inspections) over time, mutual understanding emerges as the individuals themselves better comprehend the position of the other party. As the Norwegian Coast Guard puts it:

> When we cooperate with Russian officials, Russian fishermen subsequently learn about our rules and procedures. This lowers the chance of serious violations at sea. Moreover, we learn about the Russian approach to the same issues. This helps harmonise rules and regulation across the two countries. (Østhagen 2018)

In turn, compromise is reached. As Hønneland and Jørgensen describe the 'culture of cooperation' in the Barents Sea: '[a] common feature in these cases [fisheries cooperation] is that the parties met exactly in the middle'.[3] Crucially, this 'middle' is not given, it is constructed through dialogue and communication (Risse 2000). The same can be said about the Barents 2010 maritime delimitation treaty, where the parties divided the disputed area almost exactly in half, after four decades of negotiations.

Moreover, personal relations have formed the basis for the institutionalisation of some of these mechanisms. This especially concerns the exchange of coast guard officers from Norway and Russia, as well as the formalised sharing of information and annual meetings between the Chiefs of the coast guards. This institutionalisation and its relevance for the issues at hand in the Barents Sea at large, and the FPZ specifically, played a central part in sheltering the coast guard cooperation from sanctions and restrictions put in place between Norway and Russia in 2014 (Østhagen 2016). There is thus a feedback loop taking place, between institutionalisation and personal interactions.

[3] Author's translation. Original: 'Et fellestrekk i disse sakene er at partene møttes akkurat på midten' (Hønneland and Jørgensen 2015, 67).

Bilateral Cooperation at Large

With rapidly melting sea-ice and increased maritime traffic in the region, all Arctic coastal states have placed emphasis on cooperation to help remedy some of the capacity challenges faced. This is particularly relevant for the countries' coast guards, which often constitute the bulk of—if not the only—public asset available in the maritime Arctic. The Barents Sea is therefore a remarkable case study of maritime cooperation, where Russia borders a NATO-member as well as a long-standing partner of bilateral cooperation on land as well as offshore.

Moreover, Norway is, by most definitions, a state with limited capacity and influence (Neumann et al. 2008). This is not to discount that Norway has capabilities in certain domains, where the country's reputation, wealth, and geography come into play. Yet, Norway is still Lilliputian in relation to its larger Russian neighbour (Tamnes 2011). While Norwegian security doctrine is deeply embedded in its transatlantic partnership with the United States, being a neighbour with Russia entails cooperation on everything from environmental to border issues. Neighbour relations between Norway and Russia are thus defined by having the ability to do two things at once: upholding territorial integrity and protecting sovereign rights, while also maintaining civil relations and engaging in cooperative local and regional schemes. For Norway, the Barents Sea is therefore an area of both bilateral cooperation and security concerns.

Upholding bilateral cooperation between coast guards in the face of deteriorating relations elsewhere is a consequence of the unique character of coast guards themselves, and the specific nature of the cooperative mechanisms that have developed through decades of regional interaction. Beyond the virtue of maintaining dialogue, the vitality of this specific form of cooperation lies in its intrinsic relationship with so-called 'soft' security tasks in the coast guards' role as maritime stewards, stretching beyond—and in this instance even surpassing—the military security concept.[4]

This cooperation has also been seen as a minor, yet important, component in the larger bilateral relationships with Russia, although it has received increasing attention in recent years. The differentiation between high and

[4]For a good description/overview of the various security concepts with regards to the Arctic, see Hoogensen Gjørv et al. (2014).

low politics entails a hierarchy,[5] as some policy issues undoubtedly receive more attention than others by policymakers. As such, coast guard cooperation has been kept separate from other military and security concerns through (1) regime-building between coast guards and (2) focusing on tasks related to stewardship or 'soft' security.

The bilateral maritime cooperation described above developed in tandem with the rise in activity levels in the maritime regions and the de-escalation that followed the end of the Cold War. Tasks such as fisheries inspections, emergency response, and aid to navigation go hand-in-hand with an increase in civilian maritime traffic. Therefore, central to our understanding of the coast guards, is the concept of 'soft' security tasks, moving away from a narrower definition of security revolving around the security of the state itself (Hoogensen Gjørv et al. 2014). Albeit part of the armed forces, the coast guards are arguably not primarily 'hard' security actors. Instead, they serve as the police of the sea. For example, the Norwegian coast guard reports that it spends between 60 and 70% of its resources on fisheries inspections, solely (Norwegian Government 2014).

This does not discount the role they play in military operations, when needed. Yet, on an everyday basis, the coast guards perform a whole range of tasks, most of which are civilian in nature. Consequently, as their relationship with Russia came under scrutiny in Norway after Russia's annexation of Crimea in 2014, maritime collaboration was considered indispensable (Østhagen 2016). Had the cooperation only consisted of traditional military tasks, the states would have had both less of an incentive and a more difficult time justifying continued cooperation. In the cases examined here, however, the fact that the coast guards perform a whole range of civilian tasks has sheltered them from the larger deterioration in relations that took place in other parts of the countries' military relations.

This case of bilateral cooperation between Norway and Russia in the Barents Sea—with an emphasis on the maritime domain and coast guards specifically—highlights important notions of international cooperation at sea more generally, as well as the nuances in specific coast guard cooperation in the Arctic. Next, we turn to the role of *multilateral cooperation* in these relations and in managing the range of tasks discussed in the Arctic.

[5] In 1966, Stanley Hoffmann coined the distinction between 'high' and 'low' politics, as a way of separating the different policy-spheres of European integration. Economic policy constitutes 'low politics', whereas the survival of the state, i.e. security policy, constitutes 'high politics' (Hoffman 1966, 882, 901).

References

Aftenposten. 2017. 'Russisk avis: norsk svalbardpolitikk kan føre til militær konfrontasjon.' October 5. https://www.aftenposten.no/norge/i/lBxoy/Russisk-avis-Norsk-svalbardpolitikk-kan-fore-til-militar-konfrontasjon.

Åtland, Kristian, and Kristin Ven Bruusgaard. 2009. 'When Security Speech Acts Misfire: Russia and the Elektron Incident.' *Security Dialogue* 40 (3): 333–53.

Brigham, Lawson W. 2013. 'The Fast-Changing Maritime Arctic.' In *The Fast-Changing Arctic: Rethinking Arctic Security for a Warmer World*, edited by Barry Scott Zellen, 1–17. Calgary, AB: Calgary University Press.

Byers, Michael. 2013. *International Law and the Arctic*. New York, NY: Cambridge University Press.

Checkel, Jeffrey T. 2005. 'International Institutions and Socialization in Europe: Introduction and Framework.' *International Organization* 59 (4): 801–26.

———. 2008. 'Constructivism and Foreign Policy.' In *Foreign Policy: Theories, Actors, Cases*, edited by Steve Smith, Amelia Hadfield, and Tim Dunne, 71–80. Oxford, UK: Oxford University Press.

Claes, Dag H., and Arild Moe. 2014. 'Arctic Petroleum Resources in a Regional and Global Perspective.' In *Geopolitics and Security in the Arctic: Regional Dynamics in a Global World*, edited by Rolf Tamnes and Kristine Offerdal, 97–120. London: Routledge.

Ege, Rune T. 2012. 'Norge sier nei til russisk kystvakt-samarbeid [Norway Rejects Russian Coast Guard Cooperation].' *VG*, July 23. http://www.vg.no/nyheter/innenriks/forsvaret/norge-sier-nei-til-russisk-kystvakt-samarbeid/a/10059093/.

Eie, Harald Hermansen. 2011. 'Sjøsikkerhet i det russiske Nord.' *IFS Insight*, February 1, 1–20.

Expert Commission. 2015. *Unified Effort*. Oslo: Norwegian Ministry of Defence.

Funston, Bernard. 2014. *Emergency Preparedness in Canada's North: An Examination of Community Capacity*. Toronto, ON: Walter & Duncan Foundation.

Gade, Jo, and Paal S. Hilde. 2015. 'Nordområdenes sikkerhetspolitiske betydning for NATO.' In *Norge og Russland: Sikkerhetspolitiske utfordringer i nordområdene*, edited by Tormod Heier and Anders Kjølberg, 96–110. Oslo: Universitetsforlaget.

Government Official Norway I. 2017. 'Interview: Official at Ministry of Defence I.' October 3. Oslo.

Hammerstrøm, Johan. 2015. 'Russland varsler Svalbard-bråk om nye oljeområder.' *E24*. http://e24.no/makro-og-politikk/russland/russland-varsler-svalbard-braak-om-nye-oljeomraader/23686830.

Henriksen, Tore, and Geir Ulfstein. 2010. 'Maritime Delimitation in the Arctic: The Barents Sea Treaty.' *Ocean Development & International Law* 42 (1–2): 1–21.

Hill, Christopher. 1993. 'The Capability-Expectations Gap, or Conceptualizing Europe's International Role.' *Journal of Common Market Studies* 31 (3): 305–28.

Hoffman, Stanley. 1966. 'Obstinate or Obsolete: The Fate of the Nation State and the Case of Western Europe.' *Daedalus* 95 (3): 862–915.

Holtsmark, Sven G., ed. 2015. *Naboer i frykt og forventning: Norge og Russland 1917–2014* [Neighbours in Fear and Anticipation: Norway and Russia 1917–2014]. Oslo: Pax Forlag.

Hønneland, Geir. 1999. 'Co-management and Communities in the Barents Sea Fisheries.' *Human Organization* 58 (4): 397–404.

———. 2012a. *Making Fishery Agreements Work: Post-agreement Bargaining in the Barents Sea*. Cheltenham, UK: Edward Elgar.

———. 2012b. 'Norsk-Russisk miljø- og ressursforvaltning i nordområdene.' *Nordlit*, 29. http://septentrio.uit.no/index.php/nordlit/article/view/2303/2134.

———. 2013. *Hvordan Skal Putin Ta Barentshavet Tilbake?* Bergen, Norway: Fagbokforlaget.

———. 2016. *Russia and the Arctic: Environment, Identity and Foreign Policy*. London: I.B. Tauris.

Hønneland, Geir, and Anne-Kristin Jørgensen. 2015. 'Kompromisskulturen i Barentshavet [The Culture of Compromise in the Barents Sea].' In *Norge og Russland: Sikkerhetspolitiske utfordringer i nordområdene* [Norway and Russia: Security Challenges in the High North], edited by Tormod Heier and Anders Kjølberg, 57–68. Oslo: Universitetsforlaget.

Hoogensen Gjørv, Gunhild, Dawn R. Bazely, Marina Goloviznina, and Andrew J. Tanentzap, eds. 2014. *Environmental and Human Security in the Arctic*. Abingdon, UK: Routledge.

Jacobsen, Håkon. 2014. 'Kystvakten fortsetter samarbeidet med Russland.' *NRK*. http://www.nrk.no/nordland/fortsetter-samarbeid-med-russland-1.11856338.

Jensen, Øystein. 2014. *Noreg og havets folkerett* [Norway and the Law of the Sea]. Trondheim, Norway: Akademia Forlag.

Johnston, A. I. 2001. 'Treating, International Institutions as Social Environments.' *International Studies Quarterly* 45 (4): 487–515.

Jørgensen, Jørgen Holten. 2010. *Russisk Svalbardspolitikk* [Russian Svalbard Policy]. Trondheim, Norway: Tapir Akademiske Forlag.

Kosmo, Svein. 2010. 'Kystvaktsamarbeidet Norge-Russland. En Fortsettelse Av Politikken Med Andre Midler? [Coast Guard Cooperation Norway-Russia: A Continuation of Politics Through Other Means?]' In *Forsvarets Stabsskole*, 32–33. Oslo: Norwegian Joint Staff College.

Lindi, Marte, Kristine Hirsti, Allan Klo, and Nils Mehren. 2017. 'Tilbakeviser at Russiske Styrker Har Øvd På Invasjon Av Svalbard.' *NRK*, October 18.

Lysvold, Susanne. 2010. 'Russland Og Norge Klare for Storøvelse.' *NRK*, June 1. http://www.nrk.no/nordland/russland-og-norge-klare-for-ovelse-1.7148721.

Mitchell, James R. 2013. 'The Canadian Coast Guard in Perspective.' A Paper Prepared for Action Canada, Ottawa. August. http://www.actioncanada.ca/en/wp-content/uploads/2013/08/Canadian-Coast-Guard-In-Perspective_EN.pdf.

Moe, Arild, Daniel Fjærtoft, and Indra Øverland. 2011. 'Space and Timing: Why Was the Barents Sea Delimitation Dispute Resolved in 2010?' *Polar Geography* 34 (3): 145–62.

Molenaar, Erik J. 2012. 'Fisheries Regulation in the Maritime Zones of Svalbard.' *The International Journal of Marine and Coastal Law* 27 (1): 3–58.

Neumann, Iver B., Walter Carlsnaes, John Kristen Skogan, Nina Græger, Pernille Rieker, Kristin M. Haugevik, and Stina Torjesen. 2008. *Norge og alliansene: Gamle tradisjoner, nytt spillerom.* Oslo: Norwegian Institute of International Affairs (NUPI).

Nilsen, Thomas. 2017. 'Kommersant: Russia Lists Norway's Svalbard Policy as Potential Risk of War.' *The Independent Barents Observer*, October 4. https://thebarentsobserver.com/en/security/2017/10/kommersant-russia-lists-norways-svalbard-policy-potential-risk-war.

Norwegian Coast Guard Official I. 2017. 'Interview: Norwegian Coast Guard Official.' October 1. Haakonsvern.

Norwegian Coast Guard Official II. 2017. 'Interview: Norwegian Coast Guard Leadership.' November 20. Sortland.

Norwegian Directorate of Fisheries. 2013. 'Memorandum om samarbeidsordninger om kontroll mellom det norske Fiskeridirektoratet, den norske Kystvakten, Rosrybolovstvos territorielle administrasjon for Barentshavet og Kvitsjøen og Grensedirektoratet i Russlands føderale Sikkerhetstjeneste i Murmansk.' Murmansk.

Norwegian Government. 2014. 'Kystvakten.' *Ulovlig Fiske.* https://www.regjeringen.no/no/tema/mat-fiske-og-landbruk/fiske-og-havbruk/ulovlig-fiske/kystvakten/id438806/.

Norwegian Ministry of Justice. 2009. 'St. Meld. Nr. 22 (2008–2009): Svalbard.' Oslo.

Østhagen, Andreas. 2015. 'Coastguards in Peril: A Study of Arctic Defence Collaboration.' *Defence Studies* 15 (2): 143–60.

———. 2016. 'High North, Low Politics Maritime Cooperation with Russia in the Arctic.' *Arctic Review on Law and Politics* 7 (1): 83–100.

———. 2018. 'Managing Conflict at Sea: The Case of Norway and Russia in the Svalbard Zone.' *Arctic Review on Law and Politics* 9: 100–123.

Østhagen, Andreas, and Andreas Raspotnik. 2019. 'Why Is the European Union Challenging Norway Over Snow Crab? Svalbard, Special Interests, and Arctic Governance.' *Ocean Development & International Law* 50 (2–3): 190–208.

Pedersen, Torbjørn. 2009. 'Endringer i Internasjonal Svalbard Politikk.' *Internasjonal Politikk* 67 (1): 31–44.

———. 2017. 'The Politics of Presence: The Longyearbyen Dilemma.' *Arctic Review on Law and Politics* 8: 95–108.

Pedersen, Torbjørn, and Tore Henriksen. 2009. 'Svalbard's Maritime Zones: The End of Legal Uncertainty?' *The International Journal of Marine and Coastal Law* 24 (1): 141–61.

Risse, Thomas. 2000. '"Let's Argue!": Communicative Action in World Politics.' *International Organization* 54 (1): 1–39.

Skram, Arild-Inge. 2017a. *Alltid Til Stede: Kystvakten 1997–2017* [Always Present: Coast Guard 1997–2017]. Bergen: Fagbokforlaget.

———. 2017b. 'Interview: Arild-Inge Skram, Former Chief of the Norwegian Coast Guard.' October 24. Drammen.

Stokke, Olav Schram. 2000. 'Sub-Regional Cooperation and Protection of the Arctic Marine Environment: The Barents Sea.' In *Protecting the Polar Marine Environment: Law and Policy for Pollution Prevention*, edited by Davor Vidas, 124–38. Cambridge: Cambridge University Press.

———. 2014. 'International Environmental Governance and Arctic Security.' In *Geopolitics and Security in the Arctic*, edited by Rolf Tamnes and Kristine Offerdal, 121–46. Abingdon: Routledge.

Stormark, Kjetil. 2017. 'Russland Trente På Invasjon Av Svalbard.' Aldrimer.no. https://www.aldrimer.no/russland-trente-pa-invasjon-av-svalbard/.

Svalbard Treaty. 1920. *Treaty Between Norway, the United States of America, Denmark, France, Italy, Japan, the Netherlands, Great Britain and Ireland and the British Overseas Dominions and Sweden Concerning Spitsbergen Signed in Paris 9th February 1920*. Longyearbyen: The Governor of Svalbard. http://www.sysselmannen.no/Documents/Sysselmannen_dok/English/Legacy/The_Svalbard_Treaty_9ssFy.pdf.

Tamnes, Rolf. 1997. *Oljealder 1965–1995: Norsk Utenrikspolitisk Historie*. Oslo: Cappelen Damm.

———. 2011. 'Arctic Security and Norway.' In *Arctic Security in an Age of Climate Change*, edited by James Kraska, 47–64. New York: Cambridge University Press.

Tamnes, Rolf, and Kristine Offerdal. 2014. 'Conclusion.' In *Geopolitics and Security in the Arctic: Regional Dynamics in a Global World*, edited by Rolf Tamnes and Kristine Offerdal, 166–77. Abingdon: Routledge.

Young, Oran R. 2010. 'Institutional Dynamics: Resilience, Vulnerability and Adaptation in Environmental and Resource Regimes.' *Global Environmental Change* 20 (3): 378–85.

CHAPTER 6

International Cooperation as an Arctic Solution?

Abstract Cooperation across maritime boundaries have increasingly come into focus as Arctic states attempt to tackle a growing gap between aspirations and capabilities in their respective northern waters. Multilateral cooperation has been touted as a tool to manage an increasingly challenging situation in northern waters. As the most blatant example of this, an Arctic Coast Guard Forum was officially established in 2015 after years of deliberation on its potential role. This chapter explicitly examines the notion of pan-Arctic cooperation on coast guard issues, discussing its potential and limitations. Finally, it relates these trends to general literature on international cooperation and its relevance for understanding contemporary cooperation at sea between states.

Keywords Arctic Coast Guard Forum · Arctic Council · Russia · Multilateral cooperation · Defence cooperation

As outlined in the previous chapter, cooperation across maritime boundaries have increasingly come into focus as Arctic states attempt to tackle a growing gap between aspirations and capabilities in their respective northern waters. Whereas bilateral cooperation between states is a long-standing form of alleviating some of these pressures, focus has also shifted towards multilateral circumpolar cooperation between Arctic Coast Guards, or on

A. Østhagen, *Coast Guards and Ocean Politics in the Arctic*,
https://doi.org/10.1007/978-981-15-0754-0_6

coast guard tasks. Multilateral cooperation has been touted as a tool to manage an increasingly challenging situation in northern waters.

As the most blatant example of this, an Arctic Coast Guard Forum was officially established in 2015 after years of deliberation on its potential role. Some argued that the Forum could serve as an arena to tackle security dialogue with Russia, at a time when other channels were unavailable (Conley and Rohloff 2015; Grønning 2016). Others, however, worry about attaching too much significance to the Forum, hampering practical cooperation in favour of creating yet another Arctic 'talk-shop' (Sevunts 2016). This speaks to the core concern of Arctic coast guards: namely an inherent balance between performing everyday practical tasks *and* partaking in an increasingly complex governance system in the Arctic, while their resources are under pressure.

Multilateral Coast Guard Cooperation

As the limited maritime capabilities of coastal Arctic states surfaced with the increasing national and international attention given to the Arctic, multilateral cooperation became the focal point to alleviate pressure. In 2011, the eight Arctic countries signed an agreement for search and rescue under the auspices of the Arctic Council. A similar agreement on oil spill preparedness was signed two years later, in 2013 (Arctic Council 2011, 2013). Although a sign of how Arctic states are embracing multilateral cooperation, these agreements have been criticised for having limited impact in the Arctic, mainly outlining existing responsibilities and boundaries (Rottem 2014). The coast guards themselves have also pointed out that an increased number of exercises and more regular contact between practitioners are needed to operationalise these agreements (Neffenger 2014; Joint Arctic Command 2013).

As a response, the idea of establishing a dedicated forum for Arctic coast guards was proposed (Conley et al. 2012, 37). Modelled on already existing forums for the North Pacific and the North Atlantic, American and Russian officials subsequently took the first steps towards the establishment of an 'Arctic Coast Guard Forum'. The Russian actions in Ukraine in 2014 halted the process, as representatives from the Russia were not included in two expert's meetings hosted by Canada in Sydney, NS. It was, however, decided that the chair of the Forum should follow the chairmanships of the Arctic Council. The next expert's meeting in March 2015 was therefore held in Washington, DC, and this time the Russian Coast Guard was present. The eight countries decided to push ahead, and the Arctic Coast Guard Forum (ACGF) was formally established on 30 October 2015, at the US Coast Guard Academy in New London, Connecticut (Melia 2015).

The structure of the Forum is simple. It has a rotating Chair in tandem with the Chair of the Arctic Council. The Heads of the coast guards convene annually, whereas working groups meet more frequently when needed. The working groups are concerned with tasks such as joint operations, asset sharing and increased focus on exercises. It aims at developing common situational awareness between the eight members, while also coordinating with the work being done in the Emergency Prevention, Preparedness, and Response (EPPR) working group, under the Arctic Council.

Challenges to Multilateral Coast Guard Cooperation

Although there has been great interest in forming a coast guard forum for the Arctic, there are some fundamental challenges that limit what tasks multilateral coast guard cooperation can embark on. An overarching function of most coast guards is the protection of the coastal state's sovereign rights. Coast guards uphold sovereignty through naval presence and the enforcement of national jurisdiction (Till 2004, 330–47). Fisheries inspections, for example, are an integral part of protecting a state's sovereign rights, through the management of its own marine resources. This authority cannot be shared without the coastal state ceding some of its sovereignty. Therefore, there are some limitations to the extent of collaboration within the framework of the Arctic Coast Guard Forum.

Additionally, there are significant differences between the individual coast guards operating in the Arctic region. As each coast guard is tailored to national interests, geography and institutional cultures, there is no single unified Arctic coast guard structure. The variety of mandates and structures—recapitulated in Table 6.1—consequently challenge potential dialogue of sensitive and/or of military character. As a result, the Arctic Coast Guard Forum has to resort to a 'lowest common denominator' approach (Østhagen 2015). If collaboration is to expand beyond immediate response, the relatively wide variations in mandates and competence act as a barrier. Effective defence collaboration is often dependent on a similar set of structures, with similar size and priorities (Diesen 2013; Valasek

Table 6.1 Coast guard services in the Arctic

Country	*Name*	*Organisation*	*Civilian/military*
Denmark (Greenland)	Søværnet (Navy) (1. eskadre)	Danish Defence	Military
Iceland	Landhelgisgæsla (Coast guard)	Ministry of Justice	Semi-military
Norway	Kystvakten (Coast guard)	Royal Norwegian Navy	Military
Canada	Canadian Coast Guard (CCG)	Department of Fisheries and Oceans	Civilian
USA	United States Coast Guard (USCG)	Department of Homeland Security (in peacetime)	Military/semi-military[a]
Russia	Coast Guard of the Border Service[b]	Federal Security Service (FSB)	Semi-military

Organisations with responsibility for coast guard tasks and associated institutional structures (simplified). Copied from Table 4.1 in Chapter 4

[a]The USCG is part of the US Armed Forces. Yet, it is dissimilar from the Navy and the Danish/Norwegian counterparts operating under Navy structures. As such, institutionally it straddles the categories of 'military' and 'semi-military'—a category broad in scope, which entail military attributes/affiliation, yet operating distinct from the military in peacetime

[b]In Russian: Береговая охрана ПС ФСБ России

2011). Lack of commonality in organisational structures and mandates—as shown in Table 6.1—as well as the lack of harmonisation between coast guards in the Arctic provide significant hurtles for future collaboration.

Finally, the geographic vastness of the Arctic is in itself a challenge to effective cooperation. Although this point should be self-explanatory, it tends to be overlooked in the broader public discourse, especially when politicians are making a point to praise international cooperation. Arctic geography involves large maritime domains, where few emergency incidents occur, and limited or no capabilities present. Sharing responsibility or handing over tasks to other countries is often not even an option, as states are struggling to provide sufficient capabilities in their own areas of interest. The option of practical or on-site cooperation between, for example, Norway and Canada is almost non-existent, given the great distance between these two parts of the Arctic region.

In contrast, when looking at maritime border areas with heavy seaborn traffic, like the Mediterranean Sea or the Great Lakes region, interoperability and shared tasks are more purposeful, and consequently more common.

Canadian federal police (RCMP) frequently make use of the US' Coast Guard vessels along the Great Lakes to combat drug trafficking (Canadian Coast Guard 2013). Yet, even in such border areas where cooperation is plentiful, in-depth collaboration has its limitations.

The Russian Challenge

In addition to the challenges outlined above, the integration of Russia in an Arctic Coast Guard Forum is crucial, albeit challenging. In the Bering Sea, the Chukchi Sea, and through the Bering Strait, Russia and the United States share an extensive maritime border, settled in 1990 (albeit still not ratified by the Russian Duma). Similarly, in the Barents Sea, Russia and Norway share an extensive and predominantly ice-free maritime border, settled in 2010. Finland shares a maritime border with Russia in the Gulf of Finland, though smaller in size and not in the Arctic.

In all these border areas, cooperation with Russia on both a practical as well as on a governmental level is *essential*, to effectively manage straddling fish stocks and provide environmental protection and search and rescue response.

In the initial pre-meetings for an Arctic Coast Guard Forum it became clear that Russian participation would be vital for the Forum's relevance. Partly because of Russia's extensive coastline and responsibilities along the Northeast Passage, and partly because of Russia's shared maritime borders, as outlined above. A possible expansion of coast guard collaboration in all these areas would be dependent on both diplomacy *and* cooperation with Russia. At the same time, having Russia around the table led to a bumpy start for the Forum, initially postponing its launch due to Russian actions in Ukraine in 2014.

Collaboration among all the members will have its inherent limitations due to Russia. Sensitive information cannot be shared on the same level as between the five NATO-members in the Arctic (Canada, Norway, USA, Iceland, Denmark), or even the two NATO-partners Finland and Sweden. However, how much the Forum will be hampered by the current political situation, ultimately, is dependent on the overall relationship between Russia and the other Arctic states and their willingness to keep this venue sheltered from the larger political environment in the Arctic and beyond. In most cases, coast guard affairs constitute so-called 'low politics', which states tend to separate from larger diplomatic affairs (Østhagen 2016). Furthermore, as Arctic states are increasingly looking for other venues to discuss security issues and low-level cooperation, the ACGF constitutes one step in that direction.

What Room for Manoeuvre?

Given the limitations listed above, what *can* Arctic coast guard cooperation focus on? The stated purpose, for example, of the ACGF is to further improve the relationship between the Arctic states on a *practical* level, in order to form a community focused on operational activities. This is where the aforementioned (Chapter 2) notion of epistemic communities comes into play. In a crisis, familiarity with your neighbour is crucial. For example, when a South Korean fishing vessel sank in the Bering Sea, off the Russian coast, in November 2014, the Russian Kamchatka Border Guard District requested US assistance. Several US Coast Guard assets participated in the search for survivors (Coast Guard Alaska 2014; Klint 2014). By 2019, joint patrols between the Russian and the US coast guards had taken place (Jones 2019). This example highlights the operational collaboration already taking place between the US and Russian coast guards across the Bering Strait.

The ACGF can help enhance such collaboration as activity increases. Particularly, the sharing of information and the identification of 'best practices' are areas of focus. Developing a community of experts that not only see value in sharing information and cooperating, but also develops trusts and 'socialise' into preferring collaborative solutions, has the potential to advance coast guard cooperation further. We have seen examples of these mechanisms at work on a lower level in the case of Norway-Russia in the Barents Sea.

Improving maritime situational/domain awareness and sharing information is also particularly relevant. Arctic operations are defined by limited access to communication technologies, due to the high latitude and the lack of investments in Polar-specific satellites and communication systems. Looking at defence collaboration taking place in other parts of the world, like NATO's Active Endeavour in the Mediterranean Sea, there are many ways to expand situational awareness and sharing of information. This would naturally require further agreement and harmonisation between the Arctic coastal states, particularly in regard to the difficulties concerning the inclusion of Russia.

The Arctic Coast Guard Forum is also an platform from which to initiate cross-border exercises, implementing the circumpolar agreements from 2011 to 2013 (Østhagen and Gestaldo 2015). This work is done in coordination with the Arctic Council EPPR working group (Rottem 2017). The frequency of joint contingency exercises in the Arctic has slightly increased, but a leading organisation is necessary for long-term strategic planning. The forum will also be able to provide strategic direction to emerging issues within coast guard area, in combination with the overall work that takes place under auspices of the Arctic Council or the International Maritime Organization (IMO).

Looking forward, there are some concepts that might be of interest to coast guards in the Arctic multilaterally. Pooling of resources can be utilised by coast guards, if the capacity created has relevance to more than one Arctic state. An example of pooling would be the establishment of search and rescue centres at geographically relevant locations in the Arctic. One such centre could be a Search and Rescue-unit in Keflavik, Iceland, able to rapidly conduct operations along the East coast of Greenland, north of the Faroe Islands, and in Norwegian waters around Jan Mayen, in addition to Iceland's home waters. Another example would be an oil spill response unit on Svalbard, responding to a potential spill off the coast of East Greenland (should drilling commence) or in the Barents Sea. For tasks that require immediate response, such as oil spill response or search and rescue, pooling of coast guard resources could hold value and be orchestrated by the Arctic Coast Guard Forum (Østhagen 2015).

In addition, practical cooperation on procurement of equipment seems to be an area with great potential. Here, the defence sector itself still has a long way to go, as the plethora of literature, calling for more streamlined and effective procurement policies across NATO and EU member states, indicates (Biscop and Coelmont 2012; von Voss et al. 2013). In the Arctic, potential is great among the Nordic countries, as they have relatively similar force structures, operating conditions, and they are already collaborating under the umbrella of NORDEFCO[1] (Saxi 2011; Stoltenberg 2009). The same goes for the United States and Canada, which already have a closely integrated bilateral defence cooperation under the NORAD-framework (Jockel and Sokolsky 2012). Cooperation on this level with Russia will

[1] Nordic Defense Cooperation.

have its limitations, although there could arguably be room for expansion when dealing with civilian capabilities and ice-related technology.

It is interesting to note that, whereas the more in-depth forms of collaboration prove difficult for coast guards, due to national jurisdiction and sovereignty concerns, the opposite is the case with the lighter forms of collaboration. The soft security nature of coast guard tasks works to their advantage. As a matter of fact, light collaboration between coast guards dealing with tasks of a non-sensitive nature, such as sharing of information, joint exercises, training, and procurement, could easily be facilitated. However, even among fellow NATO member states, seemingly insurmountable hurtles arise, as soon as the nature of the tasks change—more specifically, when we talk about heavier forms of military to military collaboration.

The Future of Multilateral Cooperation in the Arctic

The Arctic states and their respective coast guards are under mounting pressure. Cooperating with neighbouring coast guards—formalised through the establishment of an Arctic Coast Guard Forum (ACGF)—can help provide some remedy to these challenges. States engage in cooperation with other states to solve problems that transcend borders. Yet, when do officials and diplomats pack up their bags and leave the negotiation table? Given the development of multilateral coast guard cooperation described above, how can these efforts be best understood in conjunction with conceptualisations of *why* states cooperate?

Returning to theoretical conceptions of the underlying dynamics of why states cooperate, it seems clear that Arctic states are all better off cooperating—by sharing information, improving each other's capacities, and assisting possible emergency scenarios—than not cooperating. Yet, there is concern about the states having the ability and capacity to coordinate and capitalise on this apparent potential. The ACGF thus becomes an instrument to enable cooperation, albeit with a weak or limited structure and no enforcement mechanisms.

However, it seems clear that multilateral *pan-Arctic* coast guard cooperation between Arctic states was not developed to serve an immediate demand that states could not deal with on their own or through bilateral modes of cooperation. As shown, there are marked limitations to what can actually be achieved in a multilateral setting. Instead, the coast guards (and their respective states) seem to have realised the benefits of cooperation for the sake of cooperation and avoid a focus on 'contentious issues'. As one coast guard official discussing the Arctic Coast Guard Forum desribes the Arctic: 'An area that we can work with collegially and not as adversaries' (Melia 2015).

Cooperation is thus a goal on its own, precisely because of its value beyond just coordination of actions between the relevant actors. In this case, it is therefore not sufficient to argue that cooperation is just a rational response to meeting a growing challenge. Albeit a difficult endeavour to grasp the 'true' motivations of states (and their officials), we can conceptualise various additional reasons for the establishment of multilateral coast guard cooperation. First, the concept of 'signalling' holds relevance to this debate. Initially introduced in international relations as it relates to game theory and games with imperfect information, signalling helps explain actions that do not initially serve a specific purpose on their own (Snidal 1985; Mock 1992).

We can conceive of Arctic states' desire to signal at two different levels, where the message in both cases is clear, along the lines of: 'we are taking appropriate steps to deal with a dire situation'. Given the warning calls from scholars and experts concerning Arctic maritime emergency potential, in turn leading to political and public demands for government action,[2] setting up multilateral forums is done to *signal* that efforts are being made to alleviate the situation. On the one hand, the audience is domestic: soothing public demands for action. On the other hand, the audience is international: showcasing to other countries that the Arctic states are sufficiently managing the changing environment in the north. Especially, concerns over the Arctic described as lacking political governance structures voiced—among others—by some Members of the European Parliament as well as by some Chinese officials,[3] has triggered a response by Arctic governments emphasising and re-iterating the robustness of the Arctic regime.[4] By signalling to both external and internal actors, the Arctic states are seen as dealing

[2]See, for example, Byers (2016), Funston (2014), Ivanova (2011), and Contenta (2010).

[3]See 'European Parliament Resolution of 9 October 2008 on Arctic Governance' (2008) and Byers (2013, 125).

[4]For in-depth studies of these efforts, see Grindheim (2009), Offerdal (2010), Keil and Raspotnik (2014), Raspotnik and Østhagen (2014), Stokke (2014a), and Bekkevold and Offerdal (2014).

with an issue of growing apprehension, even if we can question to what extent a multilateral forum alleviates actual capacity concerns.

In addition, we can conceive of cooperation as having an effect beyond coordination of policies and signalling to other actors. As described in the previous chapter on the bilateral cooperation between Norway and Russia, actors partaking in international cooperation over time 'do not emerge the same'. The role of expert communities (or epistemic communities)—such as the coast guard officials, in national policymaking also cannot be underestimated. Aspirations of creating an additional layer of Arctic governance through the inclusion of another expert-dimension to the already complex Arctic system,[5] is evident from the initial conception of the Arctic Coast Guard Forum. As was argued by a US Coast Guard Vice Admiral: 'The Arctic Coast Guard Forum (ACGF) … will be a unique maritime governance group' (Neffenger 2014, 42).

It is, however, too early to conclude on the long-term effects of the Arctic Coast Guard Forum. Given its recent origin and limited scope, its potential effects are difficult to measure. Still, understanding *how* such mechanisms can serve a purpose beyond policy-coordination among partaking states, can help us better comprehend why they are set up in the first place. It thus adds another layer to an increasingly complex regional system, as the Arctic states continue to emphasise multilateral approaches to new challenges in the Arctic.

References

Arctic Council. 2011. 'Agreement on Cooperation on Aeronautical and Maritime Search and Rescue in the Arctic.' Nuuk: Arctic Council.

———. 2013. 'Agreement on Cooperation on Marine Oil Pollution, Preparedness and Response in the Arctic.' Kiruna: Emergency Prevention Preparedness and Response Working Group.

Bekkevold, Jo Inge, and Kristine Offerdal. 2014. 'Norway's High North Policy and New Asian Stakeholders.' *Strategic Analysis* 38 (6): 825–40.

Biscop, Sven, and Jo Coelmont. 2012. 'Military Capabilities: From Pooling & Sharing to a Permanent and Structured Approach.' *Egmont, Royal Institute for International Relations—Security Policy Brief*, No. 37 (September): 1–4.

Byers, Michael. 2013. *International Law and the Arctic*. New York, NY: Cambridge University Press.

[5] See Stokke (2006, 2014b), Exner-Pirot (2013), and Keil (2014).

———. 2016. 'Arctic Cruises: Fun for Tourists, Bad for the Environment.' *The Globe and Mail*, April 18. http://www.theglobeandmail.com/opinion/arctic-cruises-great-for-tourists-bad-for-the-environment/article29648307/.

Canadian Coast Guard. 2013. 'CCG Fleet: Reports.' Ottawa: Government of Canada. http://www.ccg-gcc.gc.ca/Fleet/Search.

Coast Guard Alaska. 2014. 'International Search in the Bering.' Edited by Coast Guard Alaska. Official Blog of the 17th Coast Guard District: USCG. http://alaska.coastguard.dodlive.mil/2014/12/international-search-in-the-bering/.

Conley, Heather A., Terry Toland, Jamie Kraut, and Andreas Østhagen. 2012. 'A New Security Architecture for the Arctic: An American Perspective.' *CSIS Report.* January 20. Washington, DC: Center for Strategic & International Studies (CSIS).

Conley, Heather A., and Caroline Rohloff. 2015. *The New Ice Curtain.* Washington, DC: Center for Strategic & International Studies (CSIS).

Contenta, Sandro. 2010. 'Canadians Have Their Own Oil Worries.' *Global Post: Canada.* http://www.globalpost.com/dispatch/global-green/100602/canadians-worry-about-oil-spilling-beaufort-sea?page=0,1.

Diesen, Sverre. 2013. 'Towards an Affordable European Defence and Security Policy? The Case for Extensive European Force Integration.' In *NATO's European Allies: Military Capability and Political Will*, edited by Magnus Petersson and Janne Haaland Matlary, 57–70. Basingstoke, UK: Palgrave Macmillan.

'European Parliament Resolution of 9 October 2008 on Arctic Governance.' 2008. *European Parliament: Texts Adopted.* Brussels: European Parliament. http://www.europarl.europa.eu/sides/getDoc.do?type=TA&language=EN&reference=P6-TA-2008-0474.

Exner-Pirot, Heather. 2013. 'What Is the Arctic a Case Of? The Arctic as a Regional Environmental Security Complex and the Implications for Policy.' *The Polar Journal* 3 (1): 120–35.

Funston, Bernard. 2014. 'Emergency Preparedness in Canada's North: An Examination of Community Capacity.' Toronto, ON.

Grindheim, Astrid. 2009. 'The Scramble for the Arctic? A Discourse Analysis of Norway and the EU's Strategies Towards the European Arctic.' Thesis. Oslo: Fridtjof Nansen Institute.

Grønning, Ragnhild. 2016. 'Why Military Security Should Be Kept Out of the Arctic Council.' *High North News*, June 7. http://www.highnorthnews.com/op-ed-why-military-security-should-be-kept-out-of-the-arctic-council/.

Ivanova, Maria. 2011. 'Oil Spill Emergency Preparedness in the Russian Arctic: A Study of the Murmansk Region.' *Polar Research* 30 (7285). http://www.polarresearch.net/index.php/polar/article/view/7285.

Jockel, Joseph T., and Joel J. Sokolsky. 2012. 'Continental Defence: "Like Farmers Whose Lands Have a Common Concession Line".' In *Canada's National Security in the Post-9/11 World*, edited by David McDonough, 114–36. Toronto, ON: University of Toronto Press.

Joint Arctic Command. 2013. 'SAREX Greenland Sea 2013 Final Exercise Report (FER).' Vol. 2.0. Nuuk, Greenland: Joint Arctic Command.

Jones, Bruce. 2019. 'Russian FSB Border Guard and USCG Start Joint Patrols in Bering Sea.' *Jane's 360*, June 13. https://www.janes.com/article/89226/russian-fsb-border-guard-and-uscg-start-joint-patrols-in-bering-sea.

Keil, Kathrin. 2014. 'The Arctic: A New Region of Conflict? The Case of Oil and Gas.' *Cooperation and Conflict* 49 (2): 162–190.

Keil, Kathrin, and Andreas Raspotnik. 2014. 'The European Union's Gateways to the Arctic.' *European Foreign Affairs Review* 19 (1): 101–20.

Klint, Chris. 2014. 'U.S. Coast Guard Joins Search for 54 Fishermen After Bering Sea Sinking.' *KTUU-TV*. http://www.ktuu.com/news/news/coast-guard-monitors-bering-sea-sinking-of-60person-fishing-vessel/30000826.

Melia, Michael. 2015. 'Arctic Coast Guards Pledge Co-operation at U.S. Meeting.' *CBC News: North*, October 30. http://www.cbc.ca/news/canada/north/arctic-coast-guards-pledge-co-operation-at-u-s-meeting-1.3296921.

Mock, William B. T. 1992. 'Game Theory, Signalling and International Legal Relations.' *George Washington Journal of International Law & Economics* 26: 33–60.

Neffenger, Peter V. 2014. 'Testimony of Vice Admiral Peter V. Neffenger Vice Commandant on Implementing U.S. Policy in the Arctic.' *House Coast Guard and Maritime Transportation Subcommittee*. U.S. Department of Homeland Security.

Offerdal, Kristine. 2010. 'Arctic Energy in EU Policy: Arbitrary Interest in the Norwegian High North.' *Arctic* 63 (1): 30–42.

Østhagen, Andreas. 2015. 'Coastguards in Peril: A Study of Arctic Defence Collaboration.' *Defence Studies* 15 (2): 143–60.

———. 2016. 'High North, Low Politics Maritime Cooperation with Russia in the Arctic.' *Arctic Review on Law and Politics* 7 (1): 83–100.

Østhagen, Andreas, and Vanessa Gestaldo. 2015. 'Coast Guard Co-operation in a Changing Arctic.' Toronto: Munk-Gordon Arctic Security Program. http://gordonfoundation.ca/publication/749.

Raspotnik, Andreas, and Andreas Østhagen. 2014. 'From Seal Ban to Svalbard—The European Parliament Engages in Arctic Matters.' The Arctic Institute. March.

Rottem, Svein Vigeland. 2014. 'The Arctic Council and the Search and Rescue Agreement: The Case of Norway.' *Polar Record* 50 (3): 284–92.

Rottem, Svein Vigeland. 2017. 'The Arctic Council: Challenges and Recommendations.' In *Arctic Governance: Law and Politics, Volume 1*, edited by Svein Vigeland Rottem and Ida Folkestad Soltvedt, 231–51. London: I.B. Tauris.

Saxi, Håkon Lunde. 2011. 'Nordic Defence Cooperation after the Cold War.' *Oslo Files*. March. Oslo: Norwegian Institute for Defence Studies.

Sevunts, Levon. 2016. 'Arctic Nations Deepen Coast Guard Cooperation'. *Eye on the Arctic*, June 10.

Snidal, Duncan. 1985. 'The Game Theory of International Politics.' *World Politics* 38 (1): 25–57.

Stokke, Olav Schram. 2006. 'Examing the Consequences of Arctic Institutions.' In *International Cooperation and Arctic Governance: Regime Effectiveness and Northern Region Building*, edited by Olav Schram Stokke and Geir Hønneland, 13–26. New York, NY: Routledge.

———. 2014a. 'Asian States and Arctic Governance.' *Strategic Analysis* 38 (6): 770–83.

———. 2014b. 'International Environmental Governance and Arctic Security.' In *Geopolitics and Security in the Arctic*, edited by Rolf Tamnes and Kristine Offerdal, 121–46. Abingdon: Routledge.

Stoltenberg, Thorvald. 2009. 'Nordic Cooperation in Foreign and Security Policy.' Proposals Presented to the Extraordinary Meeting of Nordic Foreign Ministers, Oslo.

Till, Geoffrey. 2004. *Seapower: A Guide for the Twenty-First Century*. London: Frank Cass.

Valasek, Tomas. 2011. 'The Case for a New Approach to About the CER Surviving Austerity the Case for a New.' Centre for European Reform, April.

von Voss, Alicia, Claudia Major, and Christian Mölling. 2013. 'The State of Defence Cooperation in Europe.' Working Paper, Stiftung Wissenschaft und Politik, Berlin. December.

CHAPTER 7

The Growing Importance of Coast Guards

Abstract This concluding chapter takes a look at what the findings showcased in this book concerning the role of coast guards, the growing importance of maritime space in politics, and the opportunities and limitations surrounding cooperation between states at sea (both bilaterally and multilaterally) hold for ocean politics more generally, as governance of marine resources and managing maritime disputes climb on the political agendas across the world. This chapter concludes that coast guard tasks and their role in cross-boundary cooperation are on the rise, not only in the Arctic but globally as oceans are increasingly on political agendas.

Keywords UNCLOS · Territorialisation · Ocean politics · Coast guards · Positive sum game

This book has explored how states make use of their respective coast guards in order to respond to a changing maritime environment, as well as develop new forms of governance structures in order to alleviate pressure to provide adequate services and capabilities in northern waters. By looking at Arctic coast guards in conjunction with what rights and responsibilities states have at sea, literature on international cooperation between states, and examples of such cooperation both bilaterally and multilaterally, it has become clear that there is a need for further cooperation across maritime boundaries in the Arctic. Moreover, coast guards themselves as a government institution

A. Østhagen, *Coast Guards and Ocean Politics in the Arctic*,
https://doi.org/10.1007/978-981-15-0754-0_7

have been shown to be central in current Arctic developments. As maritime activity is likely to increase further, and the potential for disputes or challenges arising at sea might rise s well, this institution will continue to play centre stage in the Arctic.

This concluding chapter will not attempt at summarising all the various concepts, facts and arguments laid out over the previous chapters. Instead, let us turn towards what the findings showcased here concerning (1) the role of coast guards, (2) the growing importance of maritime space in politics, and (3) the opportunities and limitations surrounding cooperation between states at sea (both bilaterally and multilaterally) hold for ocean politics more generally, as governance of marine resources and managing maritime disputes climb on the political agendas across the world.

The Role of Coast Guards

First, as is obvious when examining Arctic states, and especially the small Nordic countries Denmark, Norway, and Iceland, the importance of sheer geographic space cannot be ignored. It is apparent that the larger the maritime domain, the more need there will be for states to manage this domain. As any map of the North Atlantic displays, the size of the Canadian, Danish, Icelandic, Norwegian, and Russian EEZs in the Arctic is instructive. This is due to the simple fact that these countries all more or less lie facing relatively open bodies of ocean with few nearby opposing states limiting a full extension of the allowed 200 nautical miles economic zone. While the concept of occupation is essential in establishing title to land territory, it does not hold relevance in the maritime domain (St-Louis 2014). Thus, as in the case of Iceland, a relatively small piece of land generates a rather considerable maritime zone which needs to be administered.

What, in turn, do large maritime zones require for coastal states setting up their respective coast guards? Arguably, space itself is less important unless considered in tandem with the size of the relevant country, defined in terms of material capabilities, resources, and population. The Nordic countries in question here are *small* states, in terms of economy and population. Albeit relatively wealthy in terms of GDP per capita and human development,[1] these countries are small in capabilities compared to neighbours such as Canada, Russia, and the USA. For example, the combination of large maritime zones in need of administration and relatively limited resources—especially when the coast guards/navies took on their modern form during the first decades after WWII—yield the 'unitary' structure we see in all these NorthEast Atlantic states. As several of the coast guard and navy officials highlight in interviews, this all-purpose set-up is especially suited to small countries with a limited resource base (Danish Ministry of Defence 2016; Icelandic Coast Guard 2016; Norwegian Coast Guard Official I 2017). Crucially, Iceland is closer to a micro state then a small state, which in turn places even more restrictions on resources and ability to uphold multiple maritime institutions (Icelandic Coast Guard 2016).

Moving beyond geography, resources (of the given state), and culture, there are more relevant factors among the Arctic countries. Given the all-purpose role of most coast guards and their inclusion in each countries' defence structure, security considerations come into play. A relevant example is Norway, as it shared a direct maritime boundary with Russia. The Barents Sea—north of the European continent stretching from Norway and Russia up towards the North Pole—has been central in the relationship between these two countries. In general, the Norwegian Coast Guard—as well as naval officers and military experts in Norway—emphasise the importance of the 'grey painted ships' when performing tasks in the Norwegian EEZ and the FPZ around Svalbard (Terjesen et al. 2010). Being part of the military command chain and being armed, albeit lightly, are argued to constitute factors in the success of the Coast Guard in managing sovereign rights and keeping tensions at low levels, as the military status infer authority and respect (Kosmo 2010; Skram 2017).

At the same time, we must recognise that what coast guards primarily spend time and resources on is the protection of sovereign rights through fisheries inspections. There is a gap between security and defence-led tasks, and general resource management. This latter point is crucial, as what we are discussing with regards to states and maritime space are ***sovereign rights*** to resources in the water column and on the seabed, not the exclusive right

[1] Denmark has a GDP per capita of $48,000 (2016), Iceland $49,200 (2016), and Norway $69,200 (2016). Source: https://www.cia.gov/library/publications/the-world-factbook/rankorder/2004rank.html. Denmark ranks number 5 on the United Nations Human Development Index from 20xx, Iceland number 9, and Norway number 1. Source: http://hdr.undp.org/en/composite/HDI.

to the whole maritime territory in question. This distinction is at times either ignored in debates concerning territorial conflict, or misunderstood when discussing the conflict potential from maritime disputes.

The coast guards/navy perform multiple roles at once, to the benefit of these states with large maritime zones and varying degrees of security concerns. We therefore cannot discount such considerations when committees and officials were considering the most purposeful structure of a public branch with a mandate to roam the country's maritime zones. Setting the coast guard up as a part of the Navy, as in the case of Denmark and Norway, or as a separate branch of the Armed Forces, as in the case of the United States, seem to correspond with this obvious security need states faced and still face.

Maritime Space and International Politics

This role of coast guards, and how they are set-up to manage different domains, is increasingly coming to fore in politics concerned with the ocean and ocean governance. Three trends in particular deserve further consideration: (1) the continued institutionalisation of ocean space; (2) the growing symbolic relevance of the maritime domain; (3) and increasing function of maritime space coupled with environmental awareness and concern over the same domain.

First, the *function* of ocean space itself has expanded, with more and more resources being harvested at sea, ranging from fisheries to hydrocarbons. Several trends worth highlighting are fuelling this functional expansion. Total volumes transported by sea in 2016 were 10.3 billion tons of cargo, more than double the 4 billion tons in 1990. A considerable amount of the gas that is expected to replace oil consumption will be found in offshore reservoirs (International Energy Agency [IEA] 2017), while offshore wind-farms are increasingly becoming a source of global investment (Corbetta et al. 2015, 7). Seabed minerals are also coming to fore (Levin et al. 2016; Jaeckel et al. 2017).[2] Using ship-based extraction technology, Japan successfully mined metals from its seabed in 2017, and expects large-scale commercialisation of several offshore deposits

[2]By 2017, the International Seabed Authority had granted 28 contracts to mining companies, giving them exclusive rights to explore large parts of the continental shelf *beyond* national jurisdiction in the Pacific, Atlantic and Indian Oceans (Woody 2017). However, there are serious concerns about the environmental impacts of such activities and the lack of transparent and sufficient regulation (Jaeckel 2016; Levin et al. 2016), and calls to develop an 'exploitation code regulation' by 2020 (Woody 2017).

from 2020 onwards (Kyodo 2017).[3] Finally, straddling (and high seas) fish stocks constitute a shared resource,[4] but as Wood et al. (2008) emphasise, global fish stocks are decreasing due to overfishing, in international waters *and* within national EEZs.

Second, in conjunction with this increased preoccupation with ocean space, maritime space has been subject to extensive legalisation and a rights-based regime in favour of maritime states. A change began when *all* coastal states were awarded 200-n.m. EEZs. Maritime space previously dismissed as uninteresting suddenly became an entitlement in need of 'protection'. '[J]ust as medieval villages were eventually fenced off in response to economic change, so states in the 1970s 'fenced off' larger parts of the oceans as technological and economic change increased the uses of the oceans' (Keohane and Nye 2012, 75).

In other words: The institutionalisation of the maritime domain described here continues to prompt changes in how states engage with and perceive ocean space. From having been a 'void' to becoming a legalised space for resource exploitation and protection, the trend of the 'territorialisation' of the maritime domain as a continuing process.[5] This process did not come to an end with the legalisation of this domain in the 1980s: it is still underway today as states utilise more and more of their maritime space for resource as well as political purposes. In turn, maritime space and spatial rights have become central components of the modern state, and

[3] Other potentially valuable deposits have recently been discovered across the world ocean. In the Atlantic, British scientists discovered minerals that 'contain the scarce substance tellurium in concentrations 50,000 times higher than in deposits on land' (Shukman 2017).

[4] As an object that cannot be appropriated to any individual group and is therefore vulnerable to overexploitation by self-interested/uncoordinated individual profit-seeking behaviour (the classic 'tragedy of the commons') (Crowe 1969, 1103–4; Stuart 2013).

[5] Central here is the concept of *territoriality*: the process whereby territory (here: the ocean) is claimed by individuals or groups. 'Territoriality can be seen as the spatial expression of power and the processes of control and contestation over portions of geographic space are central concerns of political geography' (Storey 2012, 8). Studies of territory and territoriality are primarily concerned with land and the human need/desire to inhabit and control land. However, the idea of 'socialised territoriality' is relevant also for discussions of the maritime domain, as it enables the role of territory to be conceived more broadly. Sack (1986, 219) sees territoriality as a 'device to create and maintain much of the geographic context through which we experience the world and give it meaning'. In turn, once 'territories have been produced, they become spatial containers within which people are socialized' (Storey 2012, 20; see also Paasi and Prokkola 2008).

coast guards have become the way in which states are present and defend rights in this space.

This process of legalisation (or territorialisation) of maritime space for states in the twenty-first century is coupled with, or fuelled by, a third trend which affects how states and their leaders view and relate to the ocean: namely, that disputes over maritime space are increasingly entangled in domestic politics. Vasquez and Valeriano (2009, 194) describe a conflict as spiralling when it becomes infused with symbolic qualities. As shown in this book, there are actors who stand to benefit from infusing it with intangible dimensions like 'national pride' or 'being cheated out of what is ours' (Åtland and Ven Bruusgaard 2009; Hønneland 2013).[6] Maritime disputes are thus not devoid of the intangible and symbolic elements that can lead to conflicts escalating beyond the initial dispute itself. This concerns not only the economic interests of the actors involved, but also wider ideas of symbolism and identity. States (and their inhabitants) *do* care about their maritime domains, even those of limited economic value, and increasingly so. In turn tis demands that states are present in these domains, predominantly through the use of coast guards.

For example, in bilateral Norwegian/Russian relations over fisheries around Svalbard from the 1990s onwards, the domestic audience has played a central role in relations. Officials in Murmansk and representatives of the fisheries industry have attempted to infuse an intangible dimension to the underlying conflict of interests, arguing that, as compared to Soviet times, Russia was now 'weak', failing to 'protect its rights' (Åtland and Ven Bruusgaard 2009; Hønneland 2013). These attempts at agenda-setting did not succeed in spurring Moscow to escalatory actions—but they show how maritime disputes are not devoid of intangible, symbolic elements that can result in conflicts escalating beyond the dispute at hand (Østhagen 2018). When in 2005 a Russian trawler 'kidnapped' two Norwegian Coast Guard Officers and fled towards Russian waters after fishing in the waters around Svalbard, the Norwegian media were quick to broadcast the event live on national television, in turn helping to spur politicians into action (Fermann and Inderberg 2015). The *role* of maritime space in domestic politics has changed over the course of four decades—from a functional space that

[6]Interestingly, this was a prominent part of the campaign to leave the EU during the BREXIT-referendum in the UK in 2016, despite fisheries only accounting for 0.05% of the country's GDP (Lichfield 2018).

inspired limited engagement, to that of a national space requiring 'protection' and defence.

In sum, states *are* concerned with their maritime space, and increasingly so. With the sea having emerged from being literally a great blue empty space to an institutionalised policy domain, the expansion of activities taking place at sea and the growing reliance on maritime activities have resulted not only in greater importance being placed on the outcome of maritime boundary disputes, but also in shifts in the political relevance and usage of the maritime domain.

Today, oceans matter more than before for states in their power-relations vis-à-vis other states, as well as for political leaders seeking to sway domestic audiences. It is precisely in this political space that coast guards become states' foremost tool for safeguarding sovereign rights (at sea) and upholding national policies concerned with the ocean.

A Positive-Sum Game at Sea?

As outlined in Chapter 2, the maritime has—because of different qualities than land—been subject to extensive legalisation and a rights-based regime in favour of maritime states. The development of the UNCLOS-regime has awarded all coastal states rights to the resources in the most expansive way possible. Going from 12 nautical mile zones to 200 nautical mile zones in a few decades was undoubtedly a way of ensuring that 'everybody wins' (apart from landlocked states) (Bailey 1997; Brown 1981). There were, however, also voices critical to this approach when negotiations were underway, arguing for a 'global commons' approach to the oceans (Vogler 2000, 48–63). This would entail that states jointly managed (under the UN) the oceans, to avoid disastrous consequences 'for the future of mankind' (Pardo 1968, 223).

From a purely 'rationalist' view, if the goal was to preserve fisheries and marine biomass, awarding states exclusive rights through extended economic zones has arguably not proven the most effective approach. As Wood et al. (2008) showcase, global fish stocks are decreasing due to overfishing both in international waters *and* within countries' EEZs. On the other hand, the EEZ is a key contributing factor in managing maritime disputes. States are keenly interested in safeguarding their extended rights at sea as specified under UNCLOS. By having an international legal regime that awards states extensive rights at sea, states themselves are eager to uphold and defend the very same regime.[7] Engaging in conflict that could endanger this regime might in turn be a poor long-term strategy for a coastal state.

Moreover, there are positive-sum outcomes by instilling cooperation across maritime boundaries. By settling maritime disputes, states can engage in previously sensitive resource development and possible joint extraction. Fishing rights and quota management similarly become easier to facilitate (Byers and Østhagen 2017). Clear jurisdictions of 'who has what rights' enable states to cooperate. Although the loss of space might in itself constitute a zero-sum game due to the nature of delineation (if one state acquires more of a given maritime territory, the other loses the same amount), joint management of transboundary resources that enable further development of these constitute positive-sum situations with mutual gains (VanderZwaag 2010; Ásgeirsdóttir and Steinwand 2016).

However, the process of resolving maritime disputes is not as straightforward as it might seem. The Beaufort Sea maritime dispute between Canada and the United States, for example, seems ripe for settlement (Baker and Byers 2012). The fear of being seen as 'giving away' rights to maritime resources in tandem with difficulties of convincing domestic interest groups of the positive-sum outcomes seem to be the main barriers in the specific case of the Beaufort Sea (Byers and Østhagen 2017). It is easier to 'manage' the dispute instead of settling it. This might not be the ideal scenario, but it can be the consequence of limited attention paid to the dispute, or not being able to attain a mutually agreeable outcome (Byers and Østhagen 2017).

At the same time, maritime disputes seldom transform into outright conflict. This in turn is explained also by the rationale driving much of the expansion in cooperation between states, namely the inherent win-win opportunities for states at sea. According to rationalist logic, cooperation can be the product of discord. In other words, states cooperate when they disagree on an issue (otherwise what is there to cooperate on?). The solution is not only limited to cooperation within the field of disagreement but recognition that sometimes formalisation and institutions are needed to overcome the self-help tendencies of the international system. Along this line of argumentation, cooperation in the maritime domain between

[7] As, for example, witnessed in the literature on potential Arctic conflicts arising over maritime zones and resources. See Moe et al. (2011), Claes and Moe (2018), Tamnes and Offerdal (2014), and Byers (2017).

states concerning shared fish stocks, oil spill response, search and rescue, and ship traffic management are formalised arrangements set-up to manage potential areas of dispute (Østhagen 2018, 112).

In other words, the reason why countries manage to keep crises at sea from escalating further, is mutual interest in preserving aspects of their cooperation; cooperation that benefits all parties. This relates to the nature of tasks at sea, as the maritime domain is of vast expanse and there are limited capabilities and resources present. Cooperation on limited assistance in the case of an emergency is thus relatively simple, spurred by the characteristics of the maritime domain. Another area of win-win opportunities lies in marine resource management (Hønneland 2012). Primarily fisheries, but also transboundary oil and gas deposits, have strong cooperative elements where it is relatively easy to recognise the need for cooperation on managing the resources.

To conclude: it has become clear from the examples in this book and the elaboration on states' rights at sea—and their growing preoccupation with the same space—that the role of coast guards in managing disputes, governing resources and in general being present in a country's maritime domain is on the rise. Coast guards have up until now been an understudied institution, often losing out to its big brother the Navy. However, as seen in contemporary developments in the Arctic, this institution is not only dealing with security and sovereignty issues on a daily basis, it is also often the only actor present in this space as changes are underway. At the same time, we have also seen how various Arctic states are struggling to maintain capacities and spending on coast guard tasks, even as the demand for their capabilities is increasing.

Coast guards are not only relevant in an Arctic context. With the domestic and international focus on the ocean as described here, states across the seven seas are investing in their coast guard structures, or re-inventing new institutions in order to protect their sovereign rights at sea. Cooperation, however, between states at sea, is not a given. Instead, it depends on states' willingness to engage in building cooperative mechanisms and institutions, and recognising the inherent benefits of working together at sea.

References

Ásgeirsdóttir, Áslaug, and Martin C. Steinwand. 2016. 'Distributive Outcomes in Contested Maritime Areas.' *Journal of Conflict Resolution* 62 (6): 1284–1313.

Åtland, Kristian, and Kristin Ven Bruusgaard. 2009. 'When Security Speech Acts Misfire: Russia and the Elektron Incident.' *Security Dialogue* 40 (3): 333–53.

Bailey, James E. 1997. 'The Unanticipated Effects of Boundaries: The Exclusive Economic Zone and Geographically Disadvantaged States Under UNCLOS III.' *Boundary and Security Bulletin* 5 (1): 87–95. http://www.dur.ac.uk/ibru/publications/view/?id=106.

Baker, James S., and Michael Byers. 2012. 'Crossed Lines: The Curious Case of the Beaufort Sea Maritime Boundary Dispute.' *Ocean Development & International Law* 43 (March 2010): 70–95.

Brown, E. D. 1981. 'Delimitation of Offshore Areas: Hard Labour and Bitter Fruits at UNCLOS III.' *Marine Policy* 5 (3): 172–84.

Byers, Michael. 2017. 'Crises and International Cooperation: An Arctic Case Study.' *International Relations* 31 (4): 375–402.

Byers, Michael, and Andreas Østhagen. 2017. 'Why Does Canada Have So Many Unresolved Maritime Boundary Disputes?' *Canadian Yearbook of International Law* 54 (October): 1–62.

Claes, Dag H., and Arild Moe. 2018. 'Arctic Offhsore Petroleum: Resources and Political Fundamentals.' In *Arctic Governance: Energy, Living Marine Resources and Shipping*, edited by Svein Vigeland Rottem, Ida Folkestad Soltvedt, and Geir Hønneland, 9–26. London: I.B. Tauris.

Corbetta, Giorgio, Andrew Ho, and Iván Pineda. 2015. 'Wind Energy Scenarios for 2030.' https://www.ewea.org/fileadmin/files/library/publications/reports/EWEA-Wind-energy-scenarios-2030.pdf.

Crowe, Beryl L. 1969. 'The Tragedy of the Commons Revisted.' *Science* 166 (3909): 1103–7.

Danish Ministry of Defence. 2016. *Forsvarsministeriets fremtidige opgaveløsning i Arktis* [Future Missions of the Danish Ministry of Defence in the Arctic]. Copenhagen, Denmark.

Fermann, Gunnar, and Tor Håkon Inderberg. 2015. 'Norway and the 2005 Elektron Affair: Conflict of Competencies and Competent Realpolitik.' In *War: An Introduction to Theories and Research on Collective Violence*, edited by Tor Georg Jakobsen, 2nd ed., 373–402. New York, NY: Nova Science.

Hønneland, Geir. 2012. *Making Fishery Agreements Work: Post-Agreement Bargaining in the Barents Sea*. Cheltenham, UK: Edward Elgar.

———. 2013. *Hvordan skal Putin ta Barentshavet tilbake?* [How Shall Putin Retake the Barents Sea?] Bergen, Norway: Fagbokforlaget.

Hopf, Ted. 2002. *Social Construction of Foreign Policy: Identities and Foreign Policies, Moscow, 1955 and 1999*. Ithaca, NY: Cornell University Press.

Huth, Paul K. 1998. *Standing Your Ground: Territorial Disputes and International Conflict*. Ann Arbor, MI: University of Michigan Press.

Icelandic Coast Guard. 2016. 'Icelandic SAR and the Coast Guard.' Interview by: Andreas Østhagen. Reykjavik.

International Energy Agency (IEA). 2017. *World Energy Outlook 2017*. Paris. https://www.iea.org/weo2017/.

Jaeckel, Aline. 2016. 'Deep Seabed Mining and Adaptive Management: The Procedural Challenges for the International Seabed Authority.' *Marine Policy* 70: 205–11.

Jaeckel, Aline, Kristina M. Gjerde, and Jeff A. Ardron. 2017. 'Conserving the Common Heritage of Humankind—Options for the Deep-Seabed Mining Regime.' *Marine Policy* 78 (November 1994): 150–57.

Keohane, Robert O., and Joseph S. Nye. 2012 (Orig. 1977). *Power and Interdependence*. 4th-Kindle ed. Boston, MA: Longman.

Kosmo, Svein. 2010. 'Kystvaktsamarbeidet Norge-Russland. En fortsettelse av politikken med andre midler? [Coast Guard Cooperation Norway-Russia: A Continuation of Politics through Other Means?].' Forsvarets Stabsskole. Oslo: Norwegian Joint Staff College.

Kyodo. 2017. 'Japan Successfully Undertakes Large-Scale Deep-Sea Mineral Extraction.' *Japantimes*, September 26. https://www.japantimes.co.jp/news/2017/09/26/national/japan-successfully-undertakes-large-scale-deep-sea-mineral-extraction/#.WlXV5qhKujt.

Levin, Lisa A., Kathryn Mengerink, Kristina M. Gjerde, Ashley A. Rowden, Cindy Lee Van Dover, Malcolm R. Clark, Eva Ramirez-Llodra, Bronwen Currie, Craig R. Smith, Kirk N. Sato, Natalya Gallo, Andrew K. Sweetman, Hannah Lily, Claire W. Armstrong, Joseph Brider. 2016. 'Defining "Serious Harm" to the Marine Environment in the Context of Deep-Seabed Mining.' *Marine Policy* 74 (September): 245–59.

Lichfield, John. 2018. 'The Brexiteers' "Take Back Our Waters" Pledge Is Meaningless Hype.' *The Guardian*, November 24. https://www.theguardian.com/commentisfree/2018/nov/23/brexit-waters-fishing-industry-eu.

Moe, Arild, Daniel Fjærtoft, and Indra Øverland. 2011. 'Space and Timing: Why Was the Barents Sea Delimitation Dispute Resolved in 2010?' *Polar Geography* 34 (3): 145–62.

Norwegian Coast Guard Official I. 2017. 'Interview: Norwegian Coast Guard Official.' October 1. Haakonsvern.

Østhagen, Andreas. 2018. 'Managing Conflict at Sea: The Case of Norway and Russia in the Svalbard Zone.' *Arctic Review on Law and Politics* 9: 100–123.

Paasi, Anssi, and Eeva Kaisa Prokkola. 2008. 'Territorial Dynamics, Cross-Border Work and Everyday Life in the Finnish-Swedish Border Area.' *Space and Polity* 12 (1): 13–29.

Pardo, Arvid. 1968. 'Address by Ambassador Arvid Pardo.' *Proceedings of the American Society of International Law at Its Annual Meeting (1921–1969)* 62 (April 25–27): 216–29.

Sack, Robert. 1986. *Human Territoriality: Its Theory and History*. Cambridge, UK: Cambridge University Press.

Shukman, David. 2017. 'Renewables' Deep-Sea Mining Conundrum.' *BBC News*, April 11. http://www.bbc.com/news/science-environment-39347620.

Skram, Arild-Inge. 2017. *Alltid til stede: Kystvakten 1997–2017* [Always Present: Coast Guard 1997–2017]. Bergen: Fagbokforlaget.

St-Louis, Carole. 2014. 'The Notion of Equity in the Determiniation of Maritime Boundaries and Its Application to the Canada–United States Boundary in the Beaufort Sea.' Thesis: Faculty of Law, University of Ottawa.

Storey, David. 2012. *Territories: The Claiming of Space*. 2nd ed. Abingdon, UK: Routledge.

Stuart, Jill. 2013. 'Regime Theory and the Study of Outer Space Politics.' E-International Relations. http://www.e-ir.info/2013/09/10/regime-theory-and-the-study-of-outer-space-politics/.

Tamnes, Rolf, and Kristine Offerdal. 2014. 'Conclusion.' In *Geopolitics and Security in the Arctic: Regional Dynamics in a Global World*, edited by Rolf Tamnes and Kristine Offerdal, 166–77. Abingdon, UK: Routledge.

Terjesen, Bjørn, Tom Kristiansen, and Roald Gjelsten. 2010. *Sjøforsvaret i krig og fred: Langs kysten og på havet gjennom 200 År* [The Navy in War and Peace: Along the Coast and at Sea Through 200 Years]. Bergen, Norway: Fagbokforlaget.

VanderZwaag, David L. 2010. 'The Gulf of Maine Boundary Dispute and Transboundary Management Challenges: Lessons to Be Learned.' *Ocean and Coastal Law Journal* 15 (2): 241–60.

Vasquez, John A., and Brandon Valeriano. 2009. 'Territory as a Source of Conflict and a Road to Peace.' In *The SAGE Handbook of Conflict Resolution*, 193–209. London: Sage.

Vogler, John. 2000. *The Global Commons: Environmental and Technological Governance*. 2nd ed. Chichester: Wiley.

Wood, Louisa J., Lucy Fish, Josh Laughren, and Daniel Pauly. 2008. 'Assessing Progress Towards Global Marine Protection Targets: Shortfalls in Information and Action.' *Oryx* 42 (3): 340–51.

Woody, Todd. 2017. 'Seabed Mining: The 30 People Who Could Decide the Fate of the Deep Ocean.' *Oceans Deeply*, September 6. https://www.newsdeeply.com/oceans/articles/2017/09/06/seabed-mining-the-24-people-who-could-decide-the-fate-of-the-deep-ocean.

Index

A. Østhagen, *Coast Guards and Ocean Politics in the Arctic*,
https://doi.org/10.1007/978-981-15-0754-0

The manufacturer's authorised representative in the EU is Springer Nature Customer Service Centre GmbH, Europaplatz 3, 69115 Heidelberg, Germany. If you have any concerns regarding our products, please contact ProductSafety@springernature.com

Printed and bound by CPI Group (UK) Ltd, Croydon, CR0 4YY
25/09/2026
02222897-0014